NOTES FROM THE MARGINS

Bending Psychoanalysis Book Series

Volume 3

 Bending
        Psychoanalysis
            Book Series

Jack Drescher, M.D.
Series Editor

NOTES FROM THE MARGINS

The Gay Analyst's Subjectivity
In the Treatment Setting

ERIC SHERMAN

THE ANALYTIC PRESS

2005   Hillsdale, NJ   London

Published by
The Analytic Press, Inc., Publishers
    Editorial Offices:
    101 West Street
    Hillsdale, NJ 07642

    www.analyticpress.com

Designed and typeset by
Christopher Jaworski, Bloomfield, NJ
qualitext@verizon.net
Typeface: Garamond 12/15

Index by Leonard Rosenbaum

An earlier version of chapter 8 was published in *Psychoanalytic Dialogues,* 12:649–666.

Library of Congress Cataloging-in-Publication Data
Sherman, Eric
    Notes from the margins : the gay analyst's subjectivity in the treatment setting / Eric Sherman
    p. cm.
    Includes bibliographical references and index
    ISBN 0–88163–411–5

Printed in the United States of America
10 9 8 7 6 5 4 3 2 1

To Dennis, for all his patience.
And to my patients, for all of theirs.

CONTENTS

ACKNOWLEDGMENTS

Many people offered invaluable assistance in the preparation of this book. I wish to thank Beth Dorfman, Caryn Sherman-Meyer, and Bruce Tuchman for their comments on various chapters, but even more for their support and encouragement. Anthony Bass and Jessica Benjamin provided invaluable supervision on some of the cases, as did members of a supervision group, Roger Rosenthal and Sharon Mariner. My thanks go to members of my study group who also provided feedback on some of the chapters: Gail Appelbaum, Gale Bayer, Elizabeth Schreiber, Alan Sirote, and especially to the group's leader, Neil Altman. Neil not only read and gave invaluable feedback on each chapter, but he served as a mentor. Finally, I could not have asked for a more supportive, guiding, respectful, and enthusiastic editor than Jack Drescher. I would never have been able to write this book had he not been so squarely in my corner from the very beginning, and for that I am eternally grateful.

FOREWORD

Eric Sherman's *Notes from the Margins* stands out for the author's openness to exposing the wide range of feelings he experiences as an analyst—a gay analyst. As recent debates around gay marriage reveal, there is still considerable feeling, in the United States at least, that homosexuality is unacceptable, contrary to the will of God, and so on. What could be more shaming than to have one's most intimate feelings characterized in this way in the mainstream culture? What are some of the implications of having a shamed identity—not just for patients, but for clinicians as well?

Helen Block Lewis (1971) pointed out that commonly analysts fail to notice when their interpretations induce shame in analysands. Lewis argued that what looked like or was interpreted as analytic resistance could often be traced to unrecognized shame. Her point was considerably amplified by Kohut and other self psychologists, so that today's analysts are far less likely to be insensitive to the shame that is endemic to the position of being an analysand and that may be intensified considerably by being the object of interpretation.

While we have made considerable progress in recognizing shame in analysands, the same cannot be said about the analyst. Of course, we now take for granted that a normally functioning analyst experiences a wide range of feelings, including shame, as part of the intersubjective situation created between the two participants in the course of analytic work. For example, it is widely recognized that patients may defend against their own feeling of shame by attempting to shame their analysts. However, it is in the nature of shameful affects that, in response to exposure, people, including analysts, tend to hide them. In ordinary clinical work, analysts may strongly defend against shame or narcissistic injury, whereas patients may go to great lengths to protect their analysts from such experience. If patients notice narcissistic vulnerability in their analysts, they may well hesitate to shame the analysts by further exposing it.

Consequent to all these factors, psychoanalytic case reports tend to underreport analysts' feelings of shame, except when those feelings can be clearly attributed to a patient's defensive operations. Shame, however, is as endemic to the role of analyst as it is to the role of patient. As Lacan (1977) pointed out, patients attribute omniscience to their analysts. Analysts may feel the need to meet the patients' demand for omniscience, and thus shame is inevitable.

Aside from the shame endemic to the roles of patient and analyst, either or both participants may be subject to shame induced by the larger society. It seems to be difficult for human beings to recognize differences among themselves without establishing a hierarchy of value, denigrating those who differ from whatever the social ideal has come to be. So people who are lower in the social hierarchy, or dark skinned, or female, or homosexual, may come to internalize the shame associated with occupying a denigrated social position. Of course, no one is immune. White male heterosexuals are also subject to shame as a function of an awareness that they have failed to live up to the social ideal of being the embodiment of strength, self-control, rationality, and so on.

Having a community in which one's feelings and identity are accepted and valued is of crucial importance, essential for defying the malignant stereotypes that are so pervasive. Sherman's *Notes from the Margins* goes a long way toward developing such a supportive community for gay analysts and therapists. His openness does a service to all of us, whatever our private sources of shame might be. He does this by being comfortable enough with his feelings of shame to reveal them in his clinical reports. He shows that openness can sometimes be an antidote to shame. In fact, in this volume, Sherman demonstrates the courage it takes to begin to challenge internal as well as external shaming forces—a necessary step if we are to be comfortable with ourselves.

Notes from the Margins is also unique in its focus on the experience of being a gay analyst, as opposed to a more objectifying focus on the gay patient. Sherman writes of his experiences, often highly anxious ones, working with heterosexual and homosexual patients, men and women. He deals with the particulars of being gay, to be sure, but the book also transcends that particularity of identity to address clinical work in the context of difference, overlapping differences and similarities in sexual orientation, gender, personality style, and more. Sherman provides a wealth of clinical experiential detail that documents what it is really like to engage with patients in this culture's highly fraught experiences of gender and sexual orientation.

Sherman provides a model of courageous and effective clinical work, while realistically recounting his failures as well as successes. There is nothing Pollyanna-like here, nor is there the usual selective emphasis on virtuoso clinical work that can intimidate a reader. This sense of real life, as opposed to the idealized—along with Sherman's self-effacing, engaging, informal, and humorous style—makes it easy for us to identify with him and draw lasting strength and inspiration from his example.

—Neil Altman

1

INTRODUCTION

Notes from the Margins is meant to defy one's usual expectations of a psychoanalytic text. The book's purpose, its format, even the way it came into being—nothing about it is traditional. It was conceived when Jack Drescher, editor of TAP's *Bending Psychoanalysis* series, invited me to dinner at a trendy (read, noisy) restaurant in Manhattan's popular Chelsea section. Over wine, Italian food, and the deafening din of dozens of conversations, we cooked up a novel idea: to do a book about what it is *really* like to work as a psychoanalyst, and specifically as a gay psychoanalyst. Toward that end, I would have to be willing to open up and show my work in all its messiness and allow myself to be vulnerable before the entire analytic community. I would need to talk about successes, failures, blind spots, and my own insecurities and countertransference quandaries. I felt both excited and frightened thinking about it.

Nevertheless, I felt compelled to take on the project. For in the last few years, two formerly overlooked and seemingly unrelated currents have captured the attention of contemporary psychoanalysts:

(1) the importance of the analyst's subjectivity as it shapes the therapeutic interaction, and (2) the role, in treatment, of patient's and therapist's gender and sexual orientation. Yet, even as books and journal articles have explored these trends, two vital areas have been largely ignored—areas that *Notes From the Margins* addresses.

First, little has been written about the unique dilemmas homosexual clinicians face when seeing patients of different genders and sexual orientations, especially gay analysts' most intimate countertransference responses. Second, too many articles, even those written within the relational perspective to which I adhere, treat the analyst's countertransference as a neat and seamless variable. Countertransference is usually presented as a feeling or attitude that the therapist can easily reflect on and overcome with just the right intervention, even in the heat of the most tense moments. In pristine clinical vignettes, confounding and disturbing enactments are miraculously worked through by the brilliant analyst's perfect response, and the treatment is forever transformed.

While this may sometimes be the case, few articles or books capture the more common and intense struggles all therapists face. Often left out is how our very humanness—our backgrounds, personalities, morals, and the personal meanings of our sexual orientation and gender—can confound, torment, and even misguide us. As a result, many working psychoanalysts may feel ashamed, inadequate, or foolish about their "imperfect" work. More troubling is that many students of psychoanalysis are given the erroneous impression that a day may eventually come when they will be free of their countertransferences—or that they can entirely master them.

This book is an attempt to correct those impressions. It does so by providing a glimpse of a gay analyst's unique subjectivity in the clinical setting. Certainly, all therapists' subjectivities are shaped by their sexual orientation and sense of gender. However, when the therapist is gay, and his history is replete with issues of secrecy, shame, alienation, difference, and internalized homophobia, he inevitably brings a unique way of listening to his patients.

By presenting detailed clinical vignettes that highlight my thoughts, feelings, personal history, and countertransference struggles with different patients, I hope to offer a glimpse inside the workings of the analyst's mind. I aim, with some trepidation, to do something quite radical: to talk about what really goes on in the treatment room—the good, the bad, the ugly, and the uncertain. Although I have highlighted particularly charged moments in several different treatments, it is important to note that the day-to-day work goes on without fanfare and outside the spotlight. Yet even during relatively quiet, stress-free moments, our subjectivity remains forever engaged. For all those clinicians who have ever felt a sense of shame about their imperfections, I hope the revelation of my own experiences can engender a feeling of freedom rather than of isolation.

As for the format of this book, theoretical and clinical material are presented separately. Chapters 3 through 9 are each devoted to telling a compelling case history, filled with action and unencumbered by immediate theoretical discussion. The clinical cases are bookended by two chapters (2 and 10) that provide the theoretical underpinnings that inform my work.

Chapter 2 begins with an examination of the role of countertransference, starting from Freud, and then focusing on contemporary models of psychoanalysis. How we understand and use our countertransference is crucial to the outcome of any treatment in the relational model. By being in touch with our own feelings toward a patient, we develop a unique understanding of the patient's complementary feelings. In this way of working, enactments are inevitable and even welcome. They provide a distinctive glimpse inside the patient's internal world, as well as into the intersubjective field cocreated by patient and therapist.

In chapter 3, the first clinical account, I present my work with José, a gay man whose effeminacy evoked discomfort and homophobia in me. The more he lisped and fluttered his hands as he spoke, the more distant and judgmental I became. As an effeminate older man, he was everything I was afraid being gay meant when I first began my own coming-out process. It was not until José challenged me during a particularly meaningful enactment that I could see just how painful— and familiar—my distancing had become for him. Working through my fears of being like José was a turning point in the treatment.

Chapter 4 highlights my work with Rich, an insecure straight man whose aggressive posturing was in stark contrast to José's "fluttery" effeminacy. Yet Rich made me feel just as insecure about my own masculinity. He and I spent much of the treatment engaging in power struggles as I worried that my homosexuality would be found out and ridiculed. Then a package delivered to my home-office brought with it a tense standoff between Rich and me.

Chapter 5 introduces the theme of sexual excitement by presenting two cases of erotic countertransference with heterosexual patients. In the first, I dissociated from my own desire for an attractive straight man for fear of being found out. As a result, he became increasingly more depressed as he undoubtedly responded to what he perceived as a lack of interest on my part.

I was much more comfortable—and flirtatious—with a seductive young heterosexual woman who had a history of coming on strong to men and then feeling spurned. By allowing myself to feel excited by her interest in me, I gave her a new experience in which sexuality and intimacy went hand-in-hand rather than being split off. Thus the patient could enter her first loving relationship—with her future husband.

In chapter 6, my fantasies about being a loving heterosexual father embroiled me in an enactment with a new mother who brought her baby to session for seven months. My failure to confront her colluded with her wish to have the perfect husband and father and to avoid her anger. When I finally confronted the patient, her hurt feelings and anger burst forth, and I was left searching for a way to welcome these new emotions without losing the patient.

In chapter 7, I present my work with a middle-aged gay virgin. Steve was so cut off from his desires that I succumbed to his sense of deadness and distance by enacting one of a therapist's (and patient's) worst nightmares—I fell asleep during a session. Rather than discuss how he felt when he saw that I was asleep, Steve was eager to ignore what had happened to avoid embarrassing both of us. Along with a number of dreams that showed his concern about whether I was truly awake and interested in him, this enactment helped me to understand better Steve's fears that his needs would go unrecognized by me, just as they had been ignored by his parents.

Chapter 8 finds me feeling aroused by a photograph a gay patient brought in of himself in a bathing suit. My mind races as I decide how to handle this important, yet uncomfortable, clinical moment. Ultimately, with much nervousness, I find a way to use my erotic feelings to help bring alive a treatment that until that point had become sanitized and barren.

Chapter 9 also touches on my sexual excitement, this time for a gay man who enacted with me his domination and submission fantasies. When Adam told me he refused to use a condom during sexual intercourse, I found out firsthand what it was like to be powerless, just as the patient felt in his real life. Ultimately, he contracted HIV, and together we had to struggle with the feelings this aroused in each of us, including anger, sadness, and self-blame.

The book's final chapter discusses specific dilemmas that the gay analyst faces in working with heterosexual and homosexual clients alike; it puts into context the clinical chapters that precede it. I examine how the gay analyst is not immune from feelings of internalized homophobia that come from growing up in a society in which being gay means one is saddled with a sense of difference and shame. How he struggles with these feelings makes all the difference between deepening the therapy and getting stuck in an impasse.

Notes from the Margins provides a glimpse of how a gay analyst uses his countertransference in his work with gay as well as straight patients. Each of the patients stirred up in me strong emotions, emotions I could not simply ignore. In presenting these cases, I hope you will get a real sense for how I understand and work with my subjectivity as it intermingles with that of the patient.

There are many challenges in writing a book that is so clinically detailed. One is to protect my patients' anonymity. While the cases in this book are all real, a number of them are composites intended to conceal the patients' identities. In all the cases, some identifying information has been changed.

Another challenge has been to make this book accessible to all readers, regardless of their sexual orientation. Every analyst—gay, bisexual, or straight—struggles with issues around shame and guilt, hiding and being seen. This book not only gives therapists permission to have these feelings, it shows them how to utilize them in the treatment.

It is my hope that this glimpse inside my consultation room stimulates discussion, self-reflection, and even criticism. As I share my own process, I hope you will feel freer to do the same. Psychoanalysis is an isolating profession. The more we have a sense of going through this together, the more we, and our patients, will benefit.

2

THE ANALYST'S SUBJECTIVITY

Working analytically requires the analyst to expose his[1] greatest vulnerabilities. Each chink in his personality armor, every insecurity, every doubt, conflict, and uncertainty, and all the ghosts from his childhood are rustled up countless times a day as he struggles to find ways to be helpful to the human beings who have entrusted him with their pain, their hopes, and their emotional well-being. It is a tall order—humbling, but also terribly exciting.

No matter how well analyzed an analyst is, his subjectivity is always alive in the room, constantly stirred by and intermingling with his patients' transferences. A therapist can find himself feeling needy with one patient, unappreciated with another, and impotent with a third. These feelings are often painfully familiar and go back to the analyst's own developmental history. The more familiar the feelings,

---

[1]In the interests of simplicity, I have chosen to use the masculine pronoun in most cases, rather than the more cumbersome "he or she."

the more likely the therapist is not to notice or to avoid them and to enact them with the patient. Yet each countertransference reaction is also shaped by the interaction with the patient and is provoked by how he needs to see the analyst as a familiar object from his own past (Mitchell, 1988). I feel needy with patient A not just because I have my own experiences of longing, but also because patient A has his own history of unmet desires. He can project that neediness into me rather than feel the painful wishes again within himself. Similarly, if patient B acts in an aloof way, his inability to recognize my subjectivity may trigger a countertransference reaction of "What about me?"

Historical Views on Countertransference

Psychoanalysis has always asked that clinicians know themselves as well as possible. However, the field's conceptualization of countertransference and ways of understanding and using a therapist's subjectivity has changed over time. Freud (1910, 1912) saw countertransference as representing unresolved unconscious conflicts and deficits in the analyst's personality. Since transference was conceptualized as distortions from the patient's past that were projected onto the analyst, the therapist, through self-analysis, needed to eliminate all personal interferences that would hinder the development and understanding of the transference. Freud (1912) believed an analyst needed to obtain a high degree of objectivity. He cautioned,

> I cannot advise my colleagues too urgently to model themselves during psychoanalytic treatment on the surgeon, who puts aside his feelings, even his human sympathy, and concentrates his mental forces on the single aim of performing the operation as skillfully as possible [p. 115].

In contrast, Freud's disciple Sándor Ferenczi (1931, 1933) argued that a patient's transference to the analyst might not be due entirely to historical distortions. In addition, not only might a therapist have a range of feelings toward his patients—such as loving and hating, seducing and disappointing—but patients are astute at discerning their analyst's countertransference.

In the 1950s, a number of writers (Heimann, 1950; Little, 1951, 1957; Benedek, 1953; Racker, 1953, 1957; Tower, 1956) took up the issue of countertransference as an inevitable consequence of the analytic situation. These writers, along with later contributors like Searles (1975) and Sandler (1976), wrote from a "totalistic" standpoint. That is to say, using a broader definition of countertransference than the original one, they saw it as a therapist's total response to the patient, both conscious and unconscious, one that takes all the analyst's personality into account.

Over time, psychoanalytic theorists began to understand countertransference as something that could be useful in the work. Many of these theorists were influenced by Kleinian thought or by that of other adherents of the British object relations school. D. W. Winnicott (1949) noted how an analyst's comfort with his hatred for the patient allowed the patient to feel more comfortable with his own aggression. Heinrich Racker (1968) labeled as a "distortion" the belief that analysis

> is an interaction between a sick person and a healthy one. The truth is that it is an interaction between two personalities. . . . each personality has external and internal dependencies, anxieties and pathological defenses; each is also a child with his internal parents; and each of these whole personalities—that of the analysand and that of the analyst—responds to every event of the analytic situation [p. 132].

Racker, however, believed that countertransference was induced by the patient and that any competent analyst would have the same countertransference with that patient: the patient's projecting his neediness into the analyst evokes a generic, infantile state of mind that would be the same in any therapist.[2] In other words, even a well-analyzed analyst would not bring his unique personality and responsiveness to the clinical encounter. If the therapist is left feeling angry, bored, judgmental, confused, seduced, or in love, it is because these feelings were placed there by the patient through projective identification. The analyst, in the words of Wilfred Bion (1959), is an empty vessel—a container—emptied of his own feelings only to be filled by those of the patient. In fact, according to Bion, the therapist's role is to provide a containing function, holding the patient's toxic projections until they can be tolerated by the patient, then feeding them back in more digestible interpretations. Bion's reworking of the relationship between a patient's projective identifications and an analyst's real-life containment of them was an important milestone in recasting this Kleinian concept as an interpersonal process.[3]

Contemporary Relational Models of Countertransference

In the component schools of what have come to be called relational models—object relations, intersubjective self psychology, interpersonal psychoanalysis, and relational psychoanalysis—the analyst's subjectivity becomes an important area of study in its own right. The analyst's countertransference is not only unavoidable, but also necessary and potentially beneficial to the treatment process.

Nevertheless, each school has its own way of understanding countertransference. The contemporary Kleinians (Pick, 1985; Spillius, 1988; Joseph, 1989) believe that a patient's projective identification

---

[2]For a discussion, see Mitchell (1997, pp. 116–117).

[3]Klein had envisioned the process of projective identification as occurring within the mind of the infant/patient, who evacuated disturbing affects into the mother/analyst *in phantasy*. The mother/analyst played little or no role in the processing of these phantasies.

finds a valence in the therapist's personality, thus introducing the analyst's particular contribution to the situation. The analyst's inability to contain projective identifications evokes his own anxieties around the patient's material, often because they mirror his own issues (Pick, 1985). When successful, the analyst uses his countertransference as a means to empathize—to comprehend what is happening within the patient by understanding what lies inside the therapist's own mind and body.

In the British Middle School (followers of Winnicott), a therapist relies on his feelings as a barometer of unformulated aspects of the patient's personality. Using his countertransference as an instrument, the analyst picks up on communications in the patient's unconscious that are felt within himself and wonders aloud with the patient what they might mean. Christopher Bollas (1987), a prominent contemporary voice in this tradition writes, "In order to find the patient we must look for him within ourselves" (p. 202). Bollas (1983) shares his own free associations, including his conflicts and how he came up with an interpretation.

> It is essential to do this because in many patients the truly free associative process takes place within the analyst, and the clinician must find some way to report his internal processes, thereby linking the patient with something he has lost in himself and enabling him to engage more authentically with the free associative process [p. 6].

Thomas Ogden (1994), an American influenced by both Winnicott and Klein, is one of the most radical thinkers in conceptualizing countertransference. Ogden uses his *reverie,* the "motley collection of psychological states that seems to reflect the analyst's narcissistic self-absorption" (p. 74), to inform his thoughts about a patient. In this approach to countertransference, the thoughts an analyst dismisses as his mind wanders in session may be precisely the thoughts of greatest importance. Ogden uses his reverie in an exciting, unconventional way in which he shows great respect for the slightest nuances of his countertransference. For example, during one session, Ogden noticed lines on an envelope on his desk that appeared to make it part of a bulk mailing. This observation led him to associate to the mechanized quality of his relationship with the patient, which he used to form an interpretation.

Intersubjectivity, an approach derived from American self psychology, examines the intersection of the subjective worlds of patient and therapist. Like self psychology, intersubjectivity relies on the analyst's countertransference as a way of experiencing empathy. If the therapist is feeling annoyed, he may wonder if the patient is feeling annoyed with him. In addition, intersubjectivity adds the concept of *organizing principles* (Stolorow and Atwood, 1992), the personalized, deeply ingrained way all people have of making sense of their inner experience. How the invariant principles of patient and analyst intersect leads either to empathy and understanding or to therapeutic breakdown and impasse. The therapist must be keenly aware of his organizing principles and his own needs and how they are being stirred up in the treatment. Bacal and Thomson (1996) write about the dangers of analysts' looking too much to patients to fill the therapists' need for mirroring and appreciation of their helpfulness. When a patient does not meet these needs, the therapist often responds by withdrawing, attacking, or making nonempathic interpretations.

In the interpersonal school, the therapist actively uses his countertransference as a way of understanding what is going on in the here-and-now relationship. This knowledge also includes inattended or dissociated aspects of their interactions that the therapist and patient may be colluding to ignore. Interpersonalists are much more likely than others to use actively—and disclose—their countertransference to confront patients about the impact they are having on the analysts. Ehrenberg (1992), for example, writes,

> The goal is to make it possible for anxieties, feelings, and fears about contact to be identified and addressed, rather than

smoothed over and obscured. . . . As reactions to intimacy and distance, as well as fears and fantasies about moments of emotional contact (or lack of emotional contact), are clarified, they can be worked through in the immediate interaction. For some patients, the opportunity to discover that neither participant need be damaged or diminished by the experience or expression of positive feelings and closeness is as crucial as discovering that it is possible to survive negative ones. The discovery that it is possible to talk about such feelings with the person with whom one is experiencing them can also be significant [pp. 39–41].

Among relational psychoanalysts, Irwin Z. Hoffman (1991) introduced social constructivism to the field. Hoffman posits that the analyst is no more privileged than the patient in knowing the "truth" about the analyst's own motivations at any given moment. Furthermore, the analyst contributes to the emerging transference partly on the basis of his individual personality. The result is that patient and therapist cocreate a relationship in which the analyst must always be skeptical that he knows all the layers of meaning he is conveying to the patient. He should instead regard the patient as a potentially astute interpreter of the countertransference. The analyst enlists the patient's feedback by asking questions ("What did you see in me?") or making statements ("I think you think I'm feeling vulnerable" or "I think you have the impression that I'm hiding my anger from you"). From this perspective, every interpretation, including a silent response, contains aspects of the analyst's subjectivity. Even if the analyst is specifically trying not to reveal something personal, he nevertheless is revealing something personal. As Aron (1996) puts it, the "analyst needs to be analyzed well enough to tolerate some degree of anxiety about having a good deal of his or her character exposed and scrutinized by patients" (p. 249).

In this model, the analyst conceptualizes countertransference as not just something induced by the patient. Just as the patient projectively identifies into the analyst, the analyst projects into the patient as well. Both have mutual influence, constantly affecting one another. The analyst enlists the patient to articulate his understanding of the analyst's actions and motivations. According to Frank (1999),

> the type of exploration I'm advising necessitates a collaborative scrutiny of the analytic interaction, attention to what is going on *between* analyst and patient. It involves the interplay of the constitutions of *both* participants, including that which is *inadvertent* on the part of both [p. 291].

Relational theorists have increasingly begun to concern themselves with a third presence in the analytic relationship. In addition to each individual's internal objects, beliefs, and predispositions, the profession of psychoanalysis always hovers in the background, sometimes out of awareness. Its sanctions and teachings and the opinions of colleagues play important roles in how we interact with our patients (Hoffman, 1994). The larger society plays a similar role, insofar as such cultural values as sexism, racism, classism, xenophobia, homophobia, and attitudes about psychoanalysis and psychotherapy have an impact on treatment (Benjamin, 1988; Altman 1996, 2000; Leary, 2000; Dimen, 2003). (This issue is taken up further in chapter 10.)

Enactments

In relational models, the analyst's ongoing work is to understand, both within himself and with the help of the patient, the forever shifting mix of feelings he is having toward the patient. He repeatedly finds himself in enactments (Levenson, 1972, 1983; Jacobs, 1986; Renik, 1988; Chused, 1991, 2003; Davies and Frawley, 1994; Frank, 1999; Bass, 2003; Black, 2003) in which some aspect of experience between the couple is put into action rather than words. The patient's personality structure, and elements from his past intermingle with the therapist's own sensibilities, history, and blind spots to create a moment of impasse, a feeling of tension, uncanniness, or uncertainty. The analyst may find himself playing out some role from the patient's life—a distant father, an abusive mother, the victimized child (Davies and Frawley, 1994). Often, the analyst may find himself or the patient playing some role from the analyst's own life, frequently without realizing it at first.

If and when the therapist "wakes up" and realizes he has become engaged in an enactment, then he may better understand what has happened and find a way out of it with the patient. This process may involve making an interpretation, an internal shift, or a self-disclosure or turning to the patient to help figure out what has been happening. Sometimes it is the patient who clues the therapist to the enactment. In either case, working through an enactment provides the analyst with a deeper understanding of the patient and the patient with the benefit of a new experience coming out of an old pattern.

Levenson (1972, 1983) and Renik (1998) believe that enactments always precede understanding of every clinical situation and that everything that happens in the therapeutic encounter is an enactment. As soon as the analyst works out of one enactment, he inevitably finds himself in the midst of another. Bass (2003) argues that distinctions should be made between major enactments and the more subtle, moment-to-moment experience. In this way, the former stand out as particularly gripping and important compared with the more common, quotidian enactments that mark each analytic session.

In my clinical work, I find enactments are unavoidable, and, in fact, they represent opportunities to propel the treatment forward. From the analyst's perspective, two common feeling states at opposite ends of the emotional spectrum may be clues that one is engaged in an enactment. One is a heightened sense of urgency, tension, unrealness. The other is a sense of deadness, boredom, or sleepiness. The analyst may forget a patient's name, schedule someone else during a patient's regular time, or suddenly be unable to remember an important fact about a client's life.

For example, with one particular patient, I had the uncanny experience that I simply could not form a coherent sentence. Relatively simple words would get stuck in my brain, and, to my chagrin, I made interpretations so long and rambling that I sometimes forgot what I was saying halfway through them. I felt mortified and stupid. What must my patient think of me? He was clearly an intelligent, well-spoken man—a Harvard graduate no less. Was I feeling intimidated or competitive? How was he being affected by his bungling therapist? And why was I acting—and feeling—so inept?

As I considered these questions, I decided to pose them to the patient. "You know," I said, "I've been having the most amazing experience with you. I'm having a hard time forming simple sentences, and I am finding myself feeling very stupid. I'm wondering if you've noticed and if you have any thoughts or reactions, including to what I just shared."

It is difficult to express how relieved I was to be able to get these sentences out without stammering or forgetting. But my relief was nothing compared with that of my patient.

"You get it!" he practically yelled. "That's exactly how I feel around people I think are smarter than me, which is just about everyone. People say I'm so intelligent, but I feel like a fraud. I've felt that way all my life."

As we spoke further, I felt my mind clear. I was fascinated by how he had communicated to me a feeling state without putting it into words. I began to think about how his impressive vocabulary and keen intellect were actually quite intimidating, and I wondered aloud whether other people found him daunting as well. Were they pulling back from embarrassment and did that contribute to the patient's experience of feeling socially ill at ease? The patient thought this was a plausible explanation. Ultimately, this enactment would lead us to take up the earliest memories of his feelings of incompetence: parents who pushed him to succeed academically, but rarely acknowledged those successes.

The Role of Shame

When supervising new therapists, I have found a frequent dynamic that makes working with enactments particularly challenging. The therapists are often highly self-critical, faulting themselves for their "mistakes," rather than seeing the context in which an enactment took place between them and their patient.

For instance, in one supervisory session, I pointed out to a supervisee who usually did a good job of staying with a patient's material that she had moved away when the patient said something subtly critical of her. The supervisee, who had not consciously realized she was being denigrated, candidly informed me that she had grown up in a household where her father was distant yet critical and her mother stood by silently. The patient had reawakened familiar feelings of inadequacy within the supervisee, without her even realizing it.

In recognition of the parallel process, I also asked if I had shamed her by pointing out her "mistake." She said she had felt somewhat embarrassed, but now that we were talking about it she felt better. This dialogue led to another question I thought we needed to consider: Had the patient felt criticized by her therapist? The supervisee thought this was likely, but it was clear that she also felt some guilt about hurting the patient in the same way she had been hurt as a child. I wondered if the patient, too, might be feeling guilty for letting the therapist down and that her guilt feelings might explain why she had criticized the supervisee in a subtle, indirect way. I wondered if there was more about the patient that we could learn from this moment. For instance, why was the patient being critical at this point? And why in a subtle, indirect way? Was she afraid of what would happen if she told her therapist directly that she was angry? Was the subtle put down designed to make the analyst feel bad about herself, and, if so, why? Did the patient have a critical, even hostile, side that both participants were colluding to avoid? Was she testing to see how the therapist would respond to guilt and criticism? What were the therapist and patient enacting from the patient's early years? Once the supervisee was able to shed her yoke of guilt sufficiently to make use of her countertransference, she was then able to think about the questions within herself and with her patient.

That example illustrates the importance of knowing oneself and one's blind spots *as much as is possible*. The goal is not to get rid of countertransference and the effects of one's personality, but to be aware of how profoundly important, and potentially beneficial, a role it plays in the treatment. This is no easy task. Understandably, when an analyst feels that shameful parts of his personality are being exposed, he may be quick to move away from the material to protect himself. The patient, sensing his analyst's discomfort, may try to protect the analyst by changing the subject or refusing to express any criticism. When such collusions take place, an opportunity to deepen the transference is temporarily lost.

Self-Disclosure

From a relational point of view, self-disclosure is not an option, but an inevitability (Aron, 1991, 1996; Greenberg, 1991, 1995; Frank, 1997; Renik, 1999). Each interpretation, question, or comment—even silence—says something about the analyst, his values, and what he thinks about the patient.

But these are inadvertent disclosures. What about the purposeful self-disclosures of countertransference reactions? Relational analysts range from extreme caution around countertransference disclosure (Ogden, 1994) to a willingness to be particularly open (Maroda, 1991; Ehrenberg, 1992; Frank, 1997; Renik, 1999). Some analysts disclose sometimes, but worry that too much disclosure robs patients of their transference fantasies and forecloses exploration (Poland, 1984; Aron, 1992, 1996; Mitchell, 1993; Epstein, 1995; Greenberg, 1995). As Greenberg (1995) points out, every disclosure reveals something about the analyst, but also conceals something else. More liberal exponents of self-disclosure believe that it encourages patients to be more curious about their analysts. Perhaps more important than what one discloses is the spirit in which the disclosure is offered and what the relationship is able to make of it. For example, is a disclosure meant to avoid a patient's anger? Is it made defensively? Does the analyst offer the information freely, or does he feel coerced? Are analyst and patient able to have an open dialogue about what it means to the patient to know this information about the analyst?

Countertransference self-disclosure should be distinguished from disclosures of personal information about the analyst (Aron, 1996). I tend to be more forthcoming about some personal disclosures (e.g., where I am going on vacation) than about others (e.g., my sexual orientation, especially to heterosexual patients—more on this subject in chapter 10). Yet I have no hard and fast rules. What guides me is my own comfort level and my sense *in the countertransference* regarding what might be most useful in advancing the treatment at a particular moment in time. If I feel coerced, or if I feel that what I might share would hurt the patient, close down inquiry, or simply make me feel uncomfortable, I am unlikely to share it. (I might, though, share that I was feeling coerced and try to understand this feeling with the patient. I would also certainly think about why I was feeling uncomfortable.) It is often impossible to know beforehand what the outcome of a countertransference disclosure will be (Aron, 1996), and so sometimes we must decide to take a carefully thought-out risk.

Self-Disclosure and the Gay or Lesbian Analyst

Self-disclosure by the analyst runs counter to traditions that say analysts should not reveal personal information. However, analysts self-disclose all the time in a performative manner (Aron, 1991; Greenberg, 1991). Even when the dyad colludes to ignore the analyst's sexual orientation, astute patients—both gay and straight—are still likely to wonder whether or not the analyst is gay.

Self-disclosure can be a particularly complicated issue for gay and lesbian analysts who presumably have already had their own experiences with coming out in the gay community. Coming out can be part of a process of relinquishing shame, reclaiming dissociated aspects of the self, experiencing new feelings of acceptance within oneself and by others, and relief at no longer having to hide (Isay, 1996; Drescher, 1998). It can mean finding a place where one finally fits in, especially when other groups, like church and family, have been nonaccepting. But some gay men and lesbians have had adverse experiences coming out, even within the gay community. Some feel pressure from gay friends to come out, including at work and to family, where the fear of rejection can be strong. Every time a gay person self-discloses, there is some fear of rejection mixed with the hope of newfound freedom and acceptance. The gay analyst's readiness to reveal his sexual orientation in treatment, and how he feels about doing this, is likely to be influenced by his own experience of coming out. Those who have never come out professionally may experience their own homosexuality as something secret and shameful (Drescher, 1998). This feeling is likely to be picked up by their patients, who have their own issues around shame.

Coming out is a form of self-disclosure that is counterintuitive to heterosexist notions of what one does and does not reveal about oneself in routine psychotherapeutic discourse. Heterosexuals do not have to announce directly that they are straight; it is automatically assumed that they are (Isay, 1991). But, by coming out, gay men and lesbians force straight people to grapple with, among other things, the issues of sex and sexuality, gender conformity, homophobia, and definitions of love and family.

When a therapist is gay, everything he says can reveal his sexual orientation, from professing knowledge of a gay bar or organization to understanding the dynamics—and the language—of gay sex. Revealing where one is going on vacation can become surprisingly complicated, particularly when one is going to a gay resort. So, to patients who (I think) do not know I am gay, I say I am vacationing on Cape

Cod. To those to whom I am out, it is Provincetown. For a gay analyst, withholding information may feel as though he is in the closet all over again (Frommer, 1999).

Yet, to avoid being found out, some gay analysts pretend not to be familiar with resources in the gay community. These therapists risk communicating to their patients that they are ashamed of being gay. This is why some gay analysts (Isay, 1991) have advocated coming out to gay patients at some point in all treatments. I, however, am uncomfortable with a "one-size-fits-all" approach to psychoanalysis. What seems more important is to try to decide what will further the treatment of a particular patient at any given moment. What does the patient want to know, why does he want to know now, and what are his conflicts around knowing?

The analyst's decision to self-disclose has different meanings for different patients. Some may experience it as seductive (Linde, 1998; Frommer, 1999). Others may feel a sense of commonality with the therapist. Some may feel special that their analyst, who usually reveals so little about himself, has chosen to share this intimate piece of information. Coming out can usher in an idealizing transference, or, for gay patients filled with shame or homophobic heterosexuals, it can lead to devaluing the analyst.

Some gay analysts find the issue of self-disclosure particularly complex when the patient is heterosexual (Keren, 1999). The analyst may worry about the patient's leaving treatment. Fears about being ridiculed or devalued by the patient may emerge from childhood memories of being taunted and shamed by straight bullies (Sherman, 2002b). Of course, they may also show a sensitivity to a homophobic patient's probable fears and reactions.

In one of the few articles written about gay analysts working with heterosexual patients, Phillips (1998) points to a dilemma that stems from the debasement of homosexuality in our society.

For the heterosexual man . . . to discover his male analyst's homosexuality places the patient in a powerful conflict: how

does he speak freely, from a virtually universal reservoir of ob-
loquy and invective, about homosexuality in general and his
analyst in particular, while simultaneously trying to maintain
the analyst's approval and regard? . . . [The] patient's fears of
divulging old prejudices about this subject that he worries will
offend the analyst . . . might . . . lead to the patient's fear of divulging his own homosexual conflicts and a wellspring of pu-
nitive condemnation surrounding them [pp. 1209–1210].

It is not surprising that, when working with heterosexual clients,
there is a danger that neither member of the dyad will want to discuss
the analyst's sexual orientation (Phillips, 1998). While gay patients are
likely to ask me directly about whether I am "one of them," heterosexual patients tend to be more inhibited. Straight male patients in
particular may be especially loath to consider that I might be gay for
fear of being involved in an intimate relationship with a gay man in
which all sorts of feelings, including sexual ones, may come up.

Conclusion

As I intend to show in the next seven chapters of clinical cases,
countertransference is the arena in which the transference comes
alive. Using our selves and our sensitivities is how we get to know our
patients and their unconscious processes in the most intimate ways.
Since the analyst is a coparticipant in enactments, the inevitability of
self-disclosures draws him as a person into the relational matrix. This
pull creates a powerful here-and-now experience that allows for the
possibility of both participants' making shifts in their internal worlds
and in the intersubjective space between them.

3

BIG BOYS DON'T CRY

Every once in a while (thankfully not too often), I have the unpleasant experience of working with a patient who, for some reason, I find annoying. Such was my experience with one of my early private patients, José, a Hispanic gay man in his late 50s.

From the beginning, I found myself having a strong reaction to José's presentation. A slight, nervous man, he talked almost nonstop and quite rapidly in a chatty, superficial way. Even more difficult for me was that he seemed to embody every homosexual stereotype. He lisped, he called other men "girl" and "she," and as he spoke his hands seemed to flutter around the room. His effeminate style made me uncomfortable because it drew attention to him as "less of a man." This stance threatened my own longstanding desire to fit into the straight male world on its masculine terms. José would not blend in, and thus called into question my own ability to be a chameleon.

José already knew something about me in a more relaxed setting. He had first met me at a workshop I gave in New York's Gay and

Lesbian Community Center on why some people repeat destructive relationship patterns. In a light, airy tone he told me that he had come to therapy to work on exactly this problem. He often found himself attracted to aggressive men. He would fall for them hard and then feel controlled by them. The same pattern was repeating itself in his current relationship. His boyfriend refused to move in with him. When they were out, the man dictated where they would go when the evening was over and whether or not they would have sex. I thought to myself, "What kind of person would stay with a man like this?" But it was clear that, as much as José complained, he had the boyfriend on a pedestal and seemed to enjoy the way their relationship worked in ways I did not yet understand but knew would be important to explore at some point. In fact, José said he had thought about leaving his lover but could never do so, any more than he could have left his previous abusive lovers. Invariably, it was always the other man who would suddenly dump José, sometimes after having been sexually unfaithful to him.

I understood little about why he kept getting into controlling relationships, and I found myself feeling annoyed with him. His whining about his relationships rather than doing something about them rubbed me the wrong way. His behavior seemed particularly passive, in a way that I unconsciously, again, associated with a particularly stereotypical effeminate stance. I had a fantasy of rolling my eyes and saying, "Oh, would you stop complaining!" I was surprised how whiny—even a little effeminate—I sounded in my own mind. I now had a better idea about why I felt so claustrophobic with José, why I frequently felt annoyed at him when he seemed to be doing nothing to cause such an intense response. Clearly I felt anger at the effeminate aspects of him that I reluctantly might be able to identify within myself. But I did not have much time to think about this, because José was talking again and I was finding it hard to think and listen at the same time. In retrospect, I wondered if part of the purpose of his rapid talking and even his effeminacy was to keep me, the powerful boyfriend/therapist, at a distance until he could decide whether he could trust me or whether I would control him as everyone else did. Was he picking up on my judgments of him? The fear of not being understood and of being judged might be driving him to talk so quickly. What had he assumed about my sexual orientation and about my reaction to his?

Having had such an uncharacteristically strong reaction of annoyance to José in the initial consultation, I was surprised nonetheless by my eagerness to work with him. Although there was a part of me that felt like dumping him, much as his boyfriends had, I was also fascinated by José's masochism and by what kept him going. There was also a part of me that felt warmly toward José, who seemed so adrift in the world. And, quite frankly, I was building a practice and needed every patient I could get.

After the session ended, I found myself thinking a lot about José and my reaction to him. Why did I have such a strong critical response? What was there about his effeminacy that was so threatening to me? I thought about my coming-out period during my late adolescence, when men like José particularly threatened me. Being gay was something that filled me with shame, and to be *that* gay—to call attention to oneself in that way—was what I feared I might be like without realizing it. Were all gay men like this? I had worried that people would see me as I now saw José, as a sad, stereotypical queen. I dreaded growing old alone, which seemed to be José's fate. In the clinical setting, I was supposed to identify with him as his therapist, although I was a gay man trying to distance myself from the very qualities José embodied.

While I had grown much more comfortable about myself as a gay person by the time I met with José, obviously there were still remnants of these feelings into which José was tapping. I did not know if my sadistic wish to slap him around and make him more of a man had anything to do with a fantasy he might have to slap around his boyfriends and be more aggressive and manly. In addition to his effeminacy, I realized I was responding to his controlling nature, since he would not let me get a word in edgewise. Maybe he also wished to slap me around—or to be slapped around by me. But, again, why the need to control or be controlled?

Getting in touch with my countertransference helped me to understand José somewhat and to pull away less. However, I continued to find myself feeling annoyed with his swishiness. With his constant complaining and bitterness, he seemed as if he had stepped off the set of the movie *Boys in the Band*[1]—a generation and an experience of being gay very different from mine. Part of this annoyance had to do with the superficial tone of his presentation. It was one thing that he lisped and waved his hands when he talked. It was another that he seemed to be talking almost to avoid silence. And what he had to say often seemed to lack much substance. Session after session he simply complained about his boyfriend without seeing his own role in the relationship and without seeming to make any progress.

At first I found myself trying to be particularly active, squeezing in interpretations, asking questions, and even giving advice about his boyfriend. Partly this was a way to connect with José and respond to the neediness I felt from him. But partly it was a defense, a way to deny my discomfort and my wish to leave him. I was far less in touch with this reaction, however, than with the side of me that was trying to be helpful. From the start, José had trouble utilizing my attempts to help him. My interpretations seemed not to touch him; my advice went unheeded.

After a while, at first without even realizing it, I found myself becoming bored. The more he talked, the more I withdrew. At times I wondered if José could see what was happening. He seemed so wrapped up in himself. After a few sessions I began to think that José knew that I was withdrawing since he seemed to be talking with more urgency in order to fill the spaces. His effeminacy only seemed to increase, which had the paradoxically opposite effect of what he must

---

[1] A play later made into a movie and a gay cult classic about a group of bitter gay men who attend a birthday party. See Crowley (1968).

have wanted—it made me withdraw even more. I knew I had to say something to José so that we could explore what was happening between us and to avoid becoming intractably stuck. I commented that he seemed to be doing much more talking in sessions recently, and I wondered if it was something he had noticed and what his thoughts were about it.

José seemed immediately relieved. "I know I've been talking more, but that's because you stopped saying anything. You seem so far away. So I guess I keep talking and talking, thinking sooner or later I'll say something that will interest you."

I was impressed that José was able to tell me this; I hadn't known whether he would be able to utilize my question or feel threatened by it. Feeling more relaxed with him than ever before, I explored with José how my going "far away" had affected him and asked what he thought the reason was behind my withdrawing. He seemed uneasy with my question but finally admitted that he thought I was straight and was made uncomfortable by the fact that he was gay. He called himself a "Nellie old queen" and said this characterization made a lot of people squirm. I felt saddened by his description of himself as a "Nellie old queen," and I felt even more saddened that I had been thinking the same thing about him.

It was only by getting in touch with this sorrow and even my own shame that I could resonate with the sadness and shame José must have felt himself. Over the next few months we were able to explore José's "Nelliness" and his own mixed feelings about it. On one hand, he seemed comfortable with who he was, a self-professed effeminate gay man. He enjoyed theater, show tunes, embroidery, antiquing—all the things real men are not supposed to like in our society but that are associated so strongly by some with being gay. José delighted in the gay anthem, "I Am What I Am" from the musical *La Cage aux Folles;* and, as long as he was with another man romantically, he could be proud of himself as he was—at least to a degree. He also felt deeply ashamed of himself many times for not being more like a man.

This was not a new feeling. José had many painful memories go-ing back to grade school of being picked on for being a sissy, a homo, or even a girl. Tears trickled down his cheeks as he recounted that even his teachers seemed uncomfortable with him and discouraged him from participating in class. Often he would try to answer a ques-tion, but the teacher would not call on him. He recalled with deep shame the time he raised his hand because he had to go to the bath-room. He waved his hand hysterically and even called out the teacher's name. She yelled at him not to interrupt. José wet his pants and was humiliated as the other kids laughed at him. He cried openly as he remembered the boy who targeted him by singing, "The sissy made a sissy in his pants." I felt I had been like his teacher, trying to ig-nore him because he made me uncomfortable. Was I also really laughing at him inside?

As he told the story it was clear that José felt great pain and anger at the teacher and students, but also that he was angry at himself for being such a "sissy." His feelings of self-loathing were an exaggerated match to the feelings I had toward him for his effeminacy. Thinking this way helped me feel a bit more empathic toward José, as I could certainly identify with what it was like to be made fun of in school. I experienced this empathy as a form of projective identification. In the treatment, I had been feeling the sense of loathing and disgust toward José that he had felt for himself. My ability to sit with the feeling (at least some of the time), to make sense of it, and work through it en-abled me ultimately to "feed it back" to him in more digestible form so that he could speak for the first time about the unhappiness he felt.

José began to talk at length about the pain of his childhood. He had grown up in a small village in the Caribbean. He had had few friends and spent a lot of time by himself playing with dolls and creat-ing a fantasy world that included dressing up his younger sister's Barbie dolls. In his special world, he made things beautiful and he felt beautiful himself. José had been particularly close to his mother and enjoyed helping her in the kitchen with the baking and cleaning. Do-ing these things left him with pride and a sense of closeness.

His mother, however, would grow more distant when his father was around; she was clearly responding to the father's discomfort about having such a mama's boy as a son. José described his father as masculine and old-fashioned, a man to whom he always wanted to be close yet never could. His father loved to fish and play baseball. José found fishing to be boring and once told me, "I couldn't play baseball to save my life, nor did I really like the game." José's two brothers did like to fish, however, and the three men would spend hours together; José stayed behind with his mother to help her with the cooking and cleaning and doing the "woman's work." José longed to please his father and feel that his father was proud of him. But neither would be the case.

Instead, his father was angry, distant, and condemning of José's effeminacy. Just as José felt he was a disappointment to the old man, he was also disappointed in the man who had raised him. As early as he could remember, José was interested in fashion and current trends. His father, however, wore his hair in an old-fashioned crew cut and owned almost nothing but T-shirts. This was what being a man meant to José: being awkward, distant, locked into masculine stereotypes, and unable to show and receive love.

Not coincidentally, that is how José undoubtedly experienced me as I became the awkward, annoyed father he could neither idealize nor get close to. In the transference, José yearned for me to be the father whom he idealized and who would finally accept him as he was. Yet he was turning me into the annoyed father by his controlling, superficial nonstop talking that left me wanting to have nothing to do with him. Could I break free of this role to be another type of father?

José may also have wanted me to be more like his mother, with whom he could feel close and share common interests. Although I usually feel comfortable in the role of a mother in the transference, José's effeminacy made me feel too much like an actual woman. I had lost the ability to take on different gender roles comfortably in the transference. Once again I found José's identifying with the feminine role so threatening because it evoked identifications I preferred not to think about.

José's longing to find the father figure he could finally get close to was evident in the men he dated. His relationships were often with older men who were as controlling as his father. He would fall for them, only to be hurt and disappointed when they left him for someone else, as his father had left José to go fishing with his brothers. José complained bitterly—only to my ears it sounded more as if he were whining, another stereotypically gay response that made me uncomfortable—about his current boyfriend, an Anglo named Peter.

Like his other boyfriends, Peter decided everything about their relationship, from how money would be spent, to how their sex life would unfold. When I asked José to tell me about the sex—a topic that had never come up before—he demurred. "A lady never talks about such things," he said, fluttering his eyes. I laughed along with him—I knew the question had hit a nerve—but I still felt uncomfortable about his calling himself a lady. There is something within me that likes to keep the boundaries between the genders rigid. A man should not refer to himself as a lady.

Nonetheless, as the months went on, I found myself feeling more comfortable with José. As this happened, he began to share more of his insecurities. He was terrified of being alone, both in the present and especially as he got older. I flashed back to my own original fear about being a gay man who would grow old alone. As I heard more, I realized that José still felt and behaved like the sissified boy who was never good enough for his father and his peers and who was always teased. He disparaged himself in all sorts of ways. He was unattractive, unintelligent, unworthy of being in a healthy relationship. "I don't blame Peter for treating me like shit," he said poignantly one day. "That's what I am, isn't it?"

I was quite moved. "Is that really what you think of yourself?" I asked.

He began to cry. "I don't know what I think of myself. A lot of the time I do feel like shit."

It made me sad to hear that he felt this way about himself, and I told him so. For a moment he seemed moved by my remarks, but then he quickly changed the subject. By sharing my sadness, I believe I scared him or made him feel more ashamed, and he was quickly off talking at an unusually fast pace in an especially effeminate manner. I postulated that getting too close meant being known as the sissy he felt he was, and the other person was bound to hurt him with this information.

Although José and I were beginning to form a connection, I never felt completely comfortable around him. I sensed that we both wished to connect on an intimate level but that we were both keeping our distance. I knew that I certainly was. His still largely superficial, effeminate presentation continued to make me uncomfortable. I was concerned we were reenacting one of his relationships (including the original one with his father) in which he made do with my judgmental distance and pity. I began to think about how I was denigrating José for his so-called effeminacy and masochism, not because of some objective value system, but because I was buying into the predominant value system based on idealization of masculine agency. After all, even in the gay world, the masculine man has a higher status than the effeminate one.

Then one day José came to session and reported that Peter had dumped him suddenly. José was both irate and despondent. A man who seldom kept a check on his feelings, he was particularly emotional, and effeminate, today. Almost immediately, he began to cry. His cry quickly became a wail, loud and high-pitched, his body shaking. The more he cried, the louder he became, and I began to squirm in my seat, afraid that he would be heard in the waiting room and in the therapist's office next door. I was aware of a feeling that made me ashamed: he cries like a girl. I also was deeply embarrassed that my suitemates would hear me with what I was judgmentally considering a "histrionic man," as if José's effeminacy would reflect on me as a therapist and as a person. This judgment—and not the possibility that José might be heard by others—was my true unconscious motivation in doing what I did next. I said to José that he might wish to lower his voice since others might hear him, and I did not want him to be embarrassed. Consciously, I thought I was being sensitive to José's feelings by cautioning him that a colleague might knock on the door and complain José was disturbing a session and then José would be even more traumatized. Clearly, I was the person who really worried about being humiliated.

José glared at me. Although his eyes were filled with tears, I could see the look of hatred and hurt in them.

"You don't give a shit about my feelings. You're worried about your own feelings. You're just trying to shut me up like everybody else. Well, this is how I cry and if you don't like it, tough shit."

Perhaps for the first time in our treatment I was deeply impressed by my patient's toughness. For a man I had been seeing as an "effeminate masochist," José packed one helluva punch. He was more in touch with my dissociated motives than I was myself, and I felt great respect for him. I told José that I thought he was absolutely right and I apologized for my lack of tact. He looked more appeased than pleased. My guilt went unabated.

While José continued to cry, I thought further about why I was so uncomfortable around him. I began to think that we were more alike than I cared to admit, two gay men who had been made fun of as kids and who could both be controlling as adults. It was the José in me I was trying to silence, just as I had been trying to quash him for decades. I remembered that even when I was in school there had always been one or two kids like José who were picked on more than I—picked on or even beaten. While I never made fun of them, I was always relieved that they were the ones bearing the brunt of the humiliation. Distancing myself from them served my own psychic survival, but part of me always felt bad that I had turned my back and even relished the suffering of someone who was not very different from me.

I reflected further on the points of identification between José and me. I had been trying to ignore the shame and disgust I felt at being gay and an outsider just as José struggled with the humiliation within himself. I had both empathized with and avoided José—and a fuller exploration of the shame—because the identification was so painful and frightening for me.

I realized now that I was both impressed by José's survival skills and even envious of his freedom to be emotionally expressive in whatever form it took. Sure, he was effeminate, but at least a part of him was comfortable with who he was. In a way he felt free, and I was aware of how constrained I sometimes felt by trying to avoid appearing as a stereotype. When his hands fluttered around the room I never thought to look down at my own, cemented to the sides of my chair in a way that appeared rigid and uncomfortable. If I looked at José in a different way he could resemble a bird, flying, while I seemed terribly grounded in a rigid gender role. It had never occurred to me I might be envious of José, even as I partly empathized with the price he had to pay in being made fun of and not fitting in.

When José stopped crying, I said, "José, I was very impressed by what you said before, when I asked you to lower your voice. I thought I was trying to protect you, but you could see through that. I bet you've noticed a lot about my attitudes toward you. Is there anything more you can tell me?"

José looked nervous and even blushed. "No, nothing else. I don't want to hurt your feelings."

"Are you sure?" I asked. "My feelings weren't hurt when you told me, 'Tough shit.' I respected you for that. I think I could take, even welcome, whatever you would say."

"Well," José said nervously, "I don't think you like me. You think of me as a big old queen."

The truth hurt, but, again, something about José's honesty, his strength and directness, was refreshing.

"Unfortunately, I don't think I've given myself a chance to know you," I said. "All I've allowed myself to see is a big old queen, as you say, and not a man of grace and strength and pain."

José began to cry again, only this time I could feel his sadness without pulling away and wanting to shush him. He thanked me for my comment and told me it meant a lot to him. He asked me why people were so threatened by his effeminacy since he wasn't doing anything to hurt anyone. "I think people are threatened when their simple but comforting beliefs—that men are only masculine and women are only feminine—are questioned," I said. "An effeminate gay man scares other men who worry about their own masculinity."

José asked me directly, "Do I scare you?"

His question made me nervous. I had been self-disclosing quite a bit until now but this seemed like an even greater risk, a deeper self-disclosure. I wondered if I had made a mistake by telling him that effeminate gay men scare other men who are insecure about their own masculinity. But then I assured myself that there was no reason not to tell the truth, since we evidently had already seen it.

"In a way you have," I said about his scaring me. "Although not right now."

"But why would I scare you?"

"Maybe I'm afraid of the ways in which we are alike," I said. "There are parts of me that don't want to think of myself as a big old queen."

"Honey, you may be many things, but you ain't no queen," José said with delicious deadpan.

"How can you be so sure?"

"Because you're a real man, not like me." And now he began to cry gently again, wiping the corner of his eyes with a tissue.

When he finished crying, I said, "Maybe even a real man can have some sissy in him, and maybe he can enjoy it as you do sometimes. Does that have to make you less of a man?"

This became an important turning point in the treatment. José admitted he had never really considered himself a true man before; maybe it was possible that he was. I played with the idea of revisiting his fantasy that I was a straight man and wondering aloud why he had assumed I was, especially when he had attended my workshop at the

Gay and Lesbian Community Center. But we had covered a lot of ground that day and were running out of time. The question would just have to wait until a later session. But I wondered what would happen if I came out to him at a later time—although I never did share my sexual orientation with him.

After that session, I was worried that I might have been too self-revealing. Yet it felt like the most genuine and moving session we had had so far. It seemed important to be open about my feelings. While at first this openness made the patient anxious, ultimately he gained a new understanding about himself. After so many months of my annoyed distancing—a trait of which he was obviously aware—José needed to know that I could be warm and understand him, even be like him, or the therapy would forever become stuck.

For a while the therapy did move. José began to act more assertively both in session and in his life. For the first time, rather than complain about his boyfriend, José became angry with him for having cheated on him and even realized it was best that the relationship ended. We began to talk more about why José was always choosing and clinging to men who treated him badly. We connected this tendency to his childhood and to the father he so much wanted to be loved by but who instead rejected him.

José began making progress in the therapy and in his outside life. In the treatment, he began to show more interest in me. He said things like, "Honey, you've got to lighten up." Another positive sign was that for six months he was able to date casually without jumping into a relationship. Then an old pattern reemerged. He came in one day and announced that he he had met the perfect man. I wondered if this perfect man was as controlling as the others, but I would not immediately have a chance to find out.

As the relationship quickly deepened, José began to talk about ending therapy. As far as he was concerned, he was cured. He claimed he had found the man of his dreams—a man who was different from all the other men he dated—and he did not feel as though he was going to be a punching bag ever again. José said he was happy for the first time in his life, and he wanted a break from therapy to concentrate on his relationship and see what he could do on his own. My concern that he was ending our relationship simply because he had found another to replace it—and that he was moving quite fast again—fell on deaf ears. Two weeks later, José announced that he was moving in with his boyfriend and that he wished to end treatment for the time being.

I thought a great deal about why José was ending therapy and repeating an old relationship pattern just at the point where we had grown closest. I believe he became afraid of his dependence on me. Always before, with both his boyfriend and his father, closeness had led to pain and disappointment, and ultimately José was abandoned for another. He may have been leaving me before I had a chance to disappoint him. Now that I was more like him, he may have needed to deny that we were so much alike after all for fear that he would devalue me as his father had devalued him and as he still devalued himself.

José would return to therapy a year later, when his relationship ended as the previous one had. He was deeply ashamed, but he also seemed interested in finding out how he had made the same mistake again and why he kept repeating this pattern. That I had shared my own shame in our previous treatment may have made it safer to return. I believe he had experienced me as caring and trustworthy and was willing to risk getting hurt by opening up.

In fact, José was far more open and less superficial the second time around, and more able to work with the transference. By being alert to when they surfaced in the treatment, we were able to look more closely at some of the self-defeating patterns he had developed in his life. In sessions, I was invariably tipped off to enactments by my sudden desire to act sadistically toward him or by José's noticing that I was acting aggressively. We were then able to tie these to his childhood, particularly his relationship with his sadistic, abandoning father and the wish to be known and accepted by him. As José cried one day, "I just wanted him to love me for who I was. Was that too much to ask?"

This time José stayed in therapy for five years. During that time, we were able not only to examine the patterns of his life but also touch on his unexpressed anger. Eventually, he was able to enter a relationship in which he did not feel pushed around. It lasted three years and was the first relationship José ended when he realized he was not getting enough of his needs met. He spent the last two years of treatment hoping to get into another relationship but also growing comfortable with being alone. He admitted that at the end of the day, it was not always so bad to come home and watch some TV, read a book, or accomplish a project by himself. This time, we decided together when it was time for José to terminate. In our last session, he cried as he told me how important I had been to him. Hearing this, I became teary myself. If I had thought to say it at the time, I might have told José, "Honey, it's been a pleasure."

José forced me to look inside myself and question some of my fundamental beliefs about masculinity and femininity. What makes a man a man? (Or a woman a woman, for that matter?) What is the difference between femininity and effeminacy? José made me ask myself a lot of tough questions, but isn't that what good patients do? As it turned out, José was not only a man, he was a man I could admire.

4

ADVENTURES IN SUBURBIA
The Analyst, the Patient, and the
Package in the Waiting Room

From the moment I heard Rich's voice on my answering machine, I knew he would be a patient I could never forget.

"Hey, Eric," he said, in what sounded like a tone of remarkable bravado. "This is Rich So-and-So. Word on the street is that you're a damn good therapist. I might want to set up a meeting, but I've got a question first. So give me a call and let's talk."

I both bristled and chuckled at Rich's moxie. I had an image of a hotshot Hollywood agent speaking to me on his speakerphone (as a cosmetologist exfoliated his follicles). I had an urge to call him back and tell him I was booked. Nonetheless, I found myself seduced and intrigued. If word had gotten out about my clinical brilliance, I at least wanted to know on what street it was being discussed.

When I called Rich back, he pointedly asked me if I was one of those "mellow, do-nothing-but-sit-silently-and-occasionally-ask-how-

it-feels" kind of therapists—by which he sneeringly meant the popular perception of the silent analyst. Or would I be the passionate, involved "in-your-face, free-for-all" kind of therapist he preferred? I
found the question fair, but Rich's manner and the words he had chosen were off-putting. I told him he would probably find me to be neither, but somewhere in the middle, and that he would get a better feel
for me, and I for him, if we met for a consultation. "Okay, cool," he
said, surprising me with his response. We set up an appointment and,
upon meeting, agreed to work together once weekly. He saw no value
in coming more frequently.

The stage was set for what would be a brief, often stormy, but always fascinating treatment. I have chosen to present my work with
Rich because, while my sexual orientation was never a subject
brought expressly into the treatment, for me it always lurked in the
background—a potentially explosive, complicating presence. My
experience of Rich as an aggressive, controlling, hypermasculine
"straight guy" threatened my own sense of masculinity and gender
identity and went to the core of what it means to me to be a gay man,
especially in relation to someone like Rich. As we both battled to
out-"man" the other, my sexuality became forever implicated in the
countertransference. It was a sometimes dangerous secret that was
part of a drama in which complementary roles frequently remained
split and enacted between us.

I saw Rich in my office in a New Jersey suburb with a large gay
population. The transference–countertransference dynamics that
would soon unfold made it difficult for me to know whether he had
any knowledge, fantasy, fear, or desire of my being gay, and whether
this had had anything to do with his choosing me as a therapist. Further complicating matters was that, unlike my Greenwich Village location in a professional building, my New Jersey office is actually
the living room of my home. This location would play an important
role in what was to unfold.

As soon as he walked in, Rich asked if I lived there. I told him I
did. He made no further comments about being in my home, and I

decided it was too early to pursue it further. He immediately launched into what had brought him to treatment. He described vague feelings of unhappiness and anger and difficulty achieving the greatness he felt he should have accomplished by his advanced age; he was almost 28. That 28 was early for a midlife crisis seemed lost on him. A musician who had already achieved some success, he had recently cut his fourth alternative-rock CD. He had started recording professionally in college, after pooling loans and investments from his parents and their friends and having written, performed, produced, and distributed his first album, with a backup band.

Rich lived his life exactly as he would later describe how he drove: fast, aggressively, and a little dangerously. If a slow car was holding him back in the fast lane, he would speed up behind the car, flash his brights, and flip the other driver the finger with anger and delight.

Rich seemed in a hurry to get through life, but he was never sure why or where he was going. The completion of his latest CD found him feeling inexplicably panicked. Yet he did not seem really to want to understand and confront his fears; he wanted only to get rid of them. Rich wanted a special therapist who was willing to throw out any normal technique and find ways to shake him up. "Try scream therapy," he implored. "Beat me up." Despite my inquiring, I was not clear why he wanted me to beat him up, although I wondered if there were clues in his background.

When I asked about his childhood, Rich quickly and defensively insisted he had had a completely happy and normal youth. But, he admitted, "I know I put gauze around my memories. I never know what's what." That was all he would say on the subject for some time.

Rich struck me as a young man—a boy, really—deeply conflicted by, and held in the grips of, his parents and his past. The faster he tried to speed away from them, the more he ended up stuck in place. Despite his ambition and accomplishments, he still depended financially on his family, who were paying for the treatment and thus making their hazy presence in the room even more strongly felt.

Rich described his father as a distant, dictatorial man who was liable to fly into sudden verbal rages. When his father called him "useless" or "a failure," Rich would scream back, red-faced, defending himself but only goading the older man to further fits of rage. I believe Rich was also both defending and attacking, identifying with and trying to disidentify with his mother, with whom he said he felt close. She would stand on the periphery of their fights and beg her son to ignore his father's taunts and not make matters worse. Rich claimed he appreciated his father's toughness but identified with his poor mother, caught in the middle. So much went on during these ugly family scenes that the wounded young Rich became completely lost.

This drama was forever being played out between Rich and me. We both defended against our identifications with the weak mother figure by taking turns as the devaluing, insecure masculine presence. I especially felt caught in the role of a well-meaning but ineffectual mother, partly owing to the force of Rich's projections, but also because I was often in the grips of a countertransference reaction in which being gay felt like being less of a man. I think both of us were in the grips of feeling not masculine enough. Rich dealt with this feeling by counterphobically strutting his masculinity. On the other hand, I tried to hide any traces of my sexual identity that would make me seem like less of a man.

Rich briefly touched on another uncomfortable subject in our consultation: he admitted that he had never had a long-term relationship. Whenever he began to get close to a woman, he would find something wrong with her, be unfaithful to her, and ultimately flee. But if someone seemed like the "right one," she would dump him.

Not surprisingly, Rich struck me as misogynistic. He described most of the women he dated as a burden, a ball-and-chain who got in the way of his career goals. Real men would not allow themselves to be "ruled" by women. He divided women into two categories—those you fuck and the nice, sweet ones you marry. I cringed as he spoke, partly because of the degrading sexism involved, but also because tough jocks like Rich were the kids who had called me "faggot" in my youth.

It was not until later that day that I thought of something else: like Rich, my father had made a similar distinction between tramps and marriage material on the night I lied and told him I had just lost my virginity with a woman. That was one of the few times I won his approval, and I sensed more than ever that I had to continue hiding the sexual orientation I felt was so unmanly, presumably threatening, and unacceptable to him.

My father and the tough boys. These two disapproving internal objects—in addition to a powerful third force in the role of society's (and even our profession's) sexism and homophobia—were always in the room in Rich's devaluing, hypermasculine swagger. He chastised me for wasting his time with "touchy-feely questions" rather than giving him practical advice. Presumably, a real man would straightforwardly tell him how to pick himself up by the bootstraps, not spend time talking about his emotional state. He labeled my desire to understand his feelings as "useless," the same invective his father had used against him. In the countertransference, Rich's attacks felt "masculine"—like body blows from a prizefighter—and they stirred my anxieties about being found out as a weak, "feminine" gay man. That I saw Rich in my home only added a layer of complexity to my struggle, no doubt similar to Rich's, about hiding and being seen.

I have consciously made every effort to transform my living room into a typical psychotherapy office. I have screened it off from the rest of the house and swept personal photos from the mantel and the top of the entertainment center. The small, enclosed front porch doubles as a waiting room, and the house's original front door serves as the entrance to the consultation room. The patients' bathroom (the same bathroom my partner and I use) is in the rear. Given the setting, people are likely to ask who else lives in the house—wife, partner, children? My New Jersey patients are getting a unique glimpse into my life—from the car in the driveway, to the smell that wafts in from the kitchen, to how I decorate and landscape my home. Ferenczi (1931) once warned of the impossibility of truly hiding anything from our patients, who notice so much about our values and the way we live our lives. But it can be hard to hold on to Ferenczi's words when you are a gay therapist practicing in your home with a patient like Rich, and the desires to hide *and* to be seen are great.

For the first few months of treatment, Rich did not ask many personal questions, but soon he began to make demands. Be more creative! Stop wasting his time and tell him what to do so he could be the success he wanted! I thought about how he had told me in the consultation that he wanted me to beat him up. Some developmental experts consider engaging in rough-and-tumble play to be a biological marker distinguishing straight boys from those who grow up to be gay (Drescher, 2002). As an adult who likes roughhousing, Rich enjoyed getting up close and in the face of other guys. His notion of treatment was to have me beat him up. Would this be the only way we could have an intimate experience? Was fighting with him the one sure way to prove to him I was a real man? Or could I take his blows without retaliating or crumbling, becoming a Winnicottian "good-enough" mother *and* father (Winnicott, 1951).

Without warning, Rich started bringing in props: videos and CDs. At first it was the music of others he admired, and a little later, his own. He would only briefly talk about the CDs, even though he said they were very meaningful to him. Instead, he would insist that I put them on as background throughout the rest of the session as we talked about other things. Any attempt to analyze, empathize, or respond in any way beyond the space he was willing to allow met with annoyance. "I didn't bring this in to talk about," he would snap. "I know how much *you* love to analyze things. I brought it in to play in the background as we talk about what I want to talk about—what's important to me and my career." With another patient, I might have felt more comfortable simply noting the importance of the patient's bringing in, in a most intimate and immediate way, parts of himself he wished me to see and understand. However, Rich's demanding quality that I do as he say made acquiescing seem impossible for me.

I felt cornered, but I also realized that hearing Rich's music, even in the background, would tell me a lot about him. I nervously told him that I would give it a try. CD in hand, Rich leapt off the couch and made a beeline to the entertainment center on the other side of the room. Annoyed at his impudence, I jumped up after him and told him I would take care of it. We then had another struggle because I wanted the music at a lower volume than he did. It was as if, by remaining inactive, I felt controlled by the victimizing Rich and the supposedly passive mother begging me to accept his abusive demands. The personal concerns of each of us seemed to be coming to the fore: Rich's wish to identify with his father and my own wish not to come across as weak and "feminine." I also felt embarrassed by what I imagined this devaluing alternative music aficionado would say not only about my inexpensive stereo system, but also about my musical tastes. There were five lite-FM–style CDs already loaded. Those discs by Madonna, Cher, and k. d. lang were not only top 40, they were stereotypically gay. "Why not throw in Barbra, Bette, and some show tunes?" I could hear him sneer. Or was that the sound of my own voice?

Then I wondered about the homoerotic element in all this. Rich wanted to open my CD player and slip in his disc, perhaps to control me, but also to be known in the most intimate way. Was I threatened by Rich's attempts to get inside me? To be on top? Or had I been signaling my readiness to go into this area by engaging in our symbolic rough sex. Would things have played out differently if Rich were gay? Finally, I wondered if we were reenacting something around physical and sexual abuse from Rich's past.

Rich and I were forever engaging in power struggles. These incidents were most likely to occur at moments when he felt most vulnerable to or criticized by me—no doubt when we felt that way toward each other. Often, I could anticipate a fight coming, usually at the end of a session, as a way for Rich to deny his humiliating dependence. I have no idea if he actually suspected I was gay, but I could imagine how such a suspicion might have made his feelings of dependency all the more terrifying for an insecure, posturing macho guy like him. Many times, I was able to avoid, pull back from, or deal creatively and productively with these important power struggles. Yet, often I found myself walking right into them as if I had not seen them coming. Once pulled in, I was a worthy adversary. Digging in my heels, I would vow not to give up ground.

I knew I was responding to Rich's baiting me, his refusal to participate in any way but what I experienced to be controlling and humiliating. After a while, I began to strike back. I would say something to injure his virility in anticipation of, or retaliation for, his lunging at mine. It was as if we were both fighting for our lives. I was finally defending myself from all the faggot-baiting boys of my childhood and adolescence.

Rich's hypermasculine devaluing also brought out a mostly unconscious subtle feeling within me that I was the passive mother in the relationship. This feeling was heightened by my own association with being gay. Part of my insistence on fighting back came from a countertransference refusal to accept this humiliating role. Rich, of course, may have been coming from a similar position. He made me so anxious, however, that I was having a hard time figuring out where he was coming from.

I had many questions and theories, but few answers, about what was happening between us. Why was I so nervous about my sexuality being exposed? Why around Rich did I equate being gay with being less of a man? Did Rich sense that my difficulty disengaging from fights had something to do with my own sense of inadequacy and fear of being found out? Did he hope I *was* gay? He never once said anything about my sexual orientation; why was I so concerned that he was going to find out? I intuited that my anxieties might be saying something about his fears around his own sexuality. He might be afraid that his own manhood was inadequate and that this meant he was gay, which could explain his sexual bravado around women. What appeared to be emerging was our shared concerns about our masculinity, although our concerns took very different forms.

Our power struggles may have also been a way for Rich to express his jealousy and longing that I be the grown-up man in the relationship and he the unsuccessful boy. His questions about my house and relationship may have been his way of trying to make of me a positive male role model for his own manhood, not necessarily to find out if I am gay. After all, he was coming to me because he had been told I was a "damn good therapist." But Rich's aggressive demands, his ability to engage us repeatedly in power struggles, and my fear of being "found out" made it difficult for me to feel idealized.

When I was able to think about Rich's need to see me as a good, strong father, I could usually pull back from, or deal creatively with, these important power struggles. As they diminished and I could feel empathy for Rich's insecurities, I began to develop a surprising fondness and compassion for him. In almost imperceptible ways, his defenses were beginning to loosen. During one session, he actually talked about how he was confused about women and why he could not get into a relationship. And he recognized—actually more like boasted—that he could be competitive around other guys. He spoke with pride about defeating a friend in a three-hour music trivia contest, and engaging in arguments with guys over who was the most successful at bedding women. One girlfriend had called these "dick fights," a term he found amusing and complimentary. Yet that he also considered the description accurate showed his potential for recognizing something about which he felt insecure.

One day, with less than 10 minutes left in the session, Rich suddenly asked if I was in a relationship. He had a demanding tone that put me on the defensive. In my nervousness, I attempted to engage in a nice, safe exploration. What made him curious? Why now? What would it mean if I were or were not in a relationship? Did he think I was?

"Here we go again!" Rich groaned. "Can't you just answer a simple question." He sounded angry, yet triumphant, the same tone he used when he talked about intimidating slow drivers.

Two voices were now conversing in my brain—having their own dick fight, perhaps. "That son-of-a-bitch," screamed the angry, panicky voice. "He's giving me no room. He always does this at the very end of the session. Don't answer him. Keep asking questions and watch *him* sweat for once."

Another voice, sounding a lot like his mother, provided different supervision: "Don't fight him. That just eggs him on. Think of how much easier it will be if you just answer his question."

Then I heard a third voice. It wondered why we had so many arguments and what it meant that they were dick fights. We had become good at using our dicks as swords, both to defend against perceived masculine humiliation and to split roles between the humiliating father and weak mother. But I felt confident we could also use our dicks, and our hearts and minds, as objects of pride and connection. I thought about what the fights were warding off for both of us—in my case, the angry, scared boy yearning to be seen.

Listening to this third voice, I said to Rich, "How about this? I will answer your question directly, but will you agree to tell me your reaction when I do?"

Rich agreed. I told him I was, indeed, in a relationship. Rich quickly jumped to his next question. Am I happy in my relationship?

"Now hold on," I said. "That's a fair and important question. But we had a deal. You agreed to share your reaction first."

"I don't have a reaction," he said dismissively. "I'm glad for you if you're in a relationship and you're happy in it. Well, are you?"

We were completely out of time. I told him we would have to end and continue next time.

"Fine," he said testily. "But *you* have to bookmark it and bring it up." Little did I know the importance of the word bookmark.

A few minutes later, I walked into the waiting room. There was a book club delivery, left face up right in the middle of the room. My partner's name was clearly readable as the addressee. Since the parcel had been delivered by regular mail, I assumed the mailman had left it leaning against the door, as he usually did when there was no room in the mailbox. Could Rich have really picked up the package, looked at it, and placed it so that my partner's name would stare right at me—a way of flipping his finger at me for not answering his question? I was incensed. How would I deal with this issue next time?

Rich arrived 10 minutes late for his next session. "I know I'm late, but there was traffic, so don't go reading things into it."

"Moi?" I said. "Why, I would never do such a thing! I'm not one of those therapists who would wonder about whether it was connected to what happened with the package last week."

Rich stiffened. "What package?"

"The one I presume you left face up in the middle of the waiting room."

"Well, I think there was a package in the waiting room when I left last time, if that's what you mean. But I didn't touch it."

"You didn't put it there or look at the name and address either?"

Rich seemed annoyed and said he had no idea of what I was talking about. I told him that was odd, given the curiosity he had expressed about my life in that very session. He thought I was making a big deal over nothing. He may have been right; this incident may have been far more fraught with significance for me than for him. It was not until later that I wondered about other meanings: whether he might be expressing a desire to know more about me and my life, not just my outer wrappings; whether I was instead shaming him by drawing attention to my relationship—and to the size of my package. We had been speaking about, and engaging in, dick fights, after all.

But, in the moment, I mostly felt tricked, powerless, and vulnerable. Stuck in this familiar position, I continued doggedly and angrily to conduct an interrogation to reaffirm again my masculine potency. But then I saw Rich's look of defiance turn to hopelessness, which provoked a response in me and allowed me to make an internal shift. I told Rich that I realized that I was coming on strong and that I was definitely doing my part to engage in a dick fight. These moments, I knew, felt awful for each of us, but they might also be empowering for him, just as he had earlier described his pride in winning such struggles with other men. I told him I was still a little dubious about what he had told me about the package, but that I had been dishonest myself by trying to prove something and get even with him. I told him I felt bad about not having put my cards on the table and telling him how I felt.

Rich's agonized look disappeared and softened into something gentler, more appreciative. But then, as if catching himself, he shrugged and said, "Can I talk about what I want to talk about now?" I dejectedly said yes, but I wished I could converse with the shrug. Toward the end of the session, I made another attempt to discuss the package. I also told him that his lack of a verbal response had left me at a loss to know how he had reacted to what I had shared. But my words went nowhere. So did an attempt to follow up and listen for off-target references in his material the following week.

And yet Rich continued to become more open and vulnerable in the sessions that followed. He even began to look different: more relaxed, happier. He was beginning to look like an attractive young man to me—no longer a petulant, manic child. I felt even more confident that I was actually helping him, reaching him.

A few weeks after the package incident, Rich reported a dream, something he seldom did:

> I was pulled over by a cop for doing 90 in a 25 zone. I tried to talk my way out of it, but the cop gave me a ticket anyway. I was really annoyed at him for not buying my story and for making me even later, because I was clearly in a rush to get somewhere. He said what I was doing was too dangerous and he couldn't just turn his back. I drove off pissed, but kept to the speed limit because I didn't want him to catch me again. I'm not sure what happened next, but I think I passed a terrible accident in which another driver who had been speeding was killed and I didn't know whether anyone else was dead.

Although the dream is "rich" (please excuse the pun) in transference and other meanings, Rich had only one association. The day after the dream he had, in fact, been caught speeding and could not talk his way out of getting a ticket. The only difference was that the cop in real life was a ball buster, and the one in the dream seemed to be cool. Rich saw his dream as a premonition, a special dream for a special person. That's all it meant. Period.

Rich went on, though. That same day, he was hit by a sudden wave of sadness so intense, he spent the entire evening drinking to get rid of the knot in his stomach. Then he decided to look through his childhood diary. He found many entries of excitement and hopes for success, but also many that were filled with anxiety and disappointment. The first unhappy experience dated to the only time he failed a test in elementary school. He was afraid his father would find out, so he did not tell him. He worked doubly hard to score well on the next two tests and so did get a good grade for the course.

That said, Rich again threatened to close down immediately. I said, "Rich, I know it's hard for you to talk about your feelings of fear and disappointment. But they are what brought you into therapy, and they are so important for us to try to understand together. Something caused such a wave of sadness that you had to drink to try to avoid it. But for the first time I've seen, another part of you that knew that you had to deal with this was strong enough to push through and look at the diary, even though it made you feel sadder. I think you'd like me to be a good, understanding cop and, rather than let you speed away from this, support and encourage that part of you."

Rich reacted with surprising openness. He said he identified with the John Lennon lyrics, "Life is what happens when you're busy making other plans." He then recounted how his second-grade teacher had singled him out in front of the class and announced that Rich was so smart that only he would be excused from the upcoming test. Rich felt proud, but then humiliated when the other kids made fun of him. "I guess that wasn't really such a good thing for him to do to me, was it?" he asked.

"No," I said, empathically. "It wasn't."

The next session was incredibly powerful. Rich shared that he had cheated on a woman he had just started dating, but that for the first time he felt guilty and wanted to make it up to her. I was struck by how Rich seemed to have developed a conscience. He also spoke about how he constantly worried that he would be filled with nothing but regrets on his deathbed. I said that maybe that was why he "drove" himself so hard. Rich responded by asking me a personal question: "You seem, like me, a guy who wants to do a lot with his life. You teach. I can tell you work hard. You must think about your deathbed, right?"

This question was different from all the others. Rich did not seem to be demanding an answer. Feeling moved, rather than put on the spot, I decided to answer him directly.

"Yes, there are times I worry that I'm driving a little too fast and missing the joy of the journey. But I think I've also learned that there has to be more to life than worrying about my deathbed."

Rich seemed grateful and shared that he, too, wanted to consider slowing down a little. However, he was also worried that therapy would make him have to stop. What if therapy took away his unique creativity? What if it took away what made him special?

I still cannot say with any certainty what happened in the sessions after the package was delivered that contributed to this temporary shift in Rich and the treatment. I believe that my refusal to back down from my anger or simply accept what Rich was telling me—as his mother would have pleaded—was of great import. And, further, I avoided becoming the abusive father by taking the risk to express regret for how I had reacted. I think Rich finally saw me as feeling sufficiently strong and confident with him to take care of both of us. In so doing, I offered myself as a new role model of masculinity, one he had always hoped that I would be, an ideal he could attain. A real man can burst out of rigidly stereotypical roles of masculinity and femininity to be aggressive *and* afraid, angry *and* apologetic, insecure *and* comfortable with himself.

As often happened, Rich needed to undo what felt like a tender moment. In the very next session, he announced that he would not be returning. I was shocked and thrown back to a confused, impotent, passive position. There was no engaging him or talking him out of this decision. I am still not sure exactly what happened. Perhaps there was something about my self-disclosure. It is possible that I sped too fast, right into his shame and vulnerability. When he sensed my acceptance of his boy-state, he may have felt both hopeful and weak, causing him to flee, just as when girlfriends stirred his dependency needs. Rich's attachment to his father was great. My becoming the new father—albeit a more loving, accepting, nonabusive male—may have been too threatening.

I think it ironic that, as I was completing this chapter, my partner and I held a commitment ceremony in the backyard of the house where Rich and I fought and interacted with one another for 45 minutes every week. I thought about Rich and my fears of being outed in the treatment as I nervously anticipated wearing my commitment ring before patients who had seen my fingers only bare.

For both patient and analyst, the subjects of shame and hiding and longing to be accepted never really go away. Yet despite Rich's sudden flight, I feel I had an impact on a rigid and troubled patient. I know that he touched me. He reminded me that being a man means using all the parts of oneself, including those typically associated with the feminine, and that being gay makes one no less of a man. I hope that Rich drives back to my office one day soon—but, if he does, that he stays within the speed limit.

5

EROTIC COUNTERTRANSFERENCE WITH HETEROSEXUAL PATIENTS

The Boy with the Hair

The first thing I noticed about Jim was his athletic good looks. He was tall, at least six feet, and had straight blond hair that would intermittently flop over his blue eyes. Several times during each twice-weekly session he would take an encroaching shock of hair, push it back off his forehead, and absentmindedly run his hand through the rest of his mane in a way I found rather sensual. I could feel a little flutter every time he did it. I was so caught up in the moment, it never occurred to me to wonder if Jim knew how I felt. I did ponder if he was purposely being flirtatious, but the absentminded way he did it led me to believe that, if anything, the gesture was deeply unconscious, out of his awareness. Would I have come to the same conclusion if Jim were gay?

Still in his mid-30s, Jim not only looked athletic, he was active in a number of amateur sports. As he described an afternoon on the basketball court, I would picture him in shorts and a tank top, showing off his muscular body. There are worse ways to make a living, I would think. Worse ways indeed.

Yet my erotic feelings were evident to me only in the very beginning of treatment. As I got to know Jim, it became hard to sustain these feelings I found both exciting and enlivening. Despite his good looks, Jim presented in a detached, depressed manner that made it difficult to maintain any physical attraction to him. I soon found myself feeling like an object being talked at by a man obsessively bent on giving me all the facts. He seemed to lack any humor, any sense of connection, or any need for me to do anything beyond just breathing and maybe listening. Not exactly my idea of an erotic playground.

Not surprisingly, Jim had come into treatment complaining of vague feelings of depression—a sense of "fuzziness" he called it—and problems of intimacy in his marriage. He and his wife, married for five years, were childless and had sex only once or twice a month. Jim had cheated on his wife on a number of occasions, although he claimed these encounters were meaningless to him. Mostly they were one-night stands with women whose names he quickly forgot. The trysts usually occurred when Jim felt close to his wife or when she put demands on him for more closeness, such as the time she insisted they enter couples therapy. Jim said he went along with her to see the marriage counselor for a month rather than say no and make waves. However, he showed his less compliant feelings by sleeping with two women he had met while prowling the pickup bars during the same period. On another occasion, he had gotten involved with a coworker, and when she wanted more than just a sexual relationship, he broke off the relationship suddenly; he vowed never to make the mistake of dating a colleague again. Currently at work a woman from another department was clearly pining away for him. He had no intention of breaking his rule about coworkers, yet he found himself avoiding her rather than telling her that he was not interested. This was the way he worked, using through avoidance rather than dealing with difficult situations directly.

Twice Jim's wife had found out about his affairs and threatened to leave him. Terrified of being alone, Jim always promised never to do it again and became very attentive toward his wife. After a while, he would feel suffocated and pressured and would begin to have extramarital sex again. I thought of what might happen between us in the treatment as Jim got closer to me. Would he feel suffocated and wish to flee, possibly to another therapist?

In an obsessive way, Jim spent much of his time in the early sessions debating about whether or not to leave his wife. If he left, he reasoned, he would feel freed from the burden of having to worry about and please her. But then he would feel terribly alone. When she was out of town on business, he would initially feel a rush of excitement and freedom, but after a while he would feel a heaviness that was nearly unbearable.

Yet, except for articulating that he felt trapped in his marriage and his job, Jim was unable to identify any other feeling states within himself. He clearly seemed depressed, yet it was difficult for him to articulate why that was so. "I don't know how to discuss how I'm feeling," he said. "Nothing means anything to me. I feel numb. When people ask, 'What's going on?' it scares me. I don't know what to say."

When I was with him, I was aware of two conflicting feelings. For short periods, I felt deeply moved and connected to him. Sometimes even the sense of erotic pleasure would momentarily return. But, more often, I felt a terrible sleepiness. No matter how well I had slept the night before, no matter how much caffeine I drank, I often felt my eyelids growing heavy in session. I came to realize that one of the reasons I fixated on Jim's good looks was because little else held my interest, and it was difficult to feel awake and invigorated with him. No doubt he used his good looks to attract women with whom he had affairs. Was this attractiveness a way to draw me in but keep me from seeing his pain? Or were we both trying to cope with more painful affect through the use of sexual feelings? Because of the deadening way in which he presented himself, it was hard to sense the terror he felt when he got too close to others or too far away.

Jim described a childhood devoid of much loving contact with others. His father, whom he described as a ne'er-do-well, left the family when Jim was five years old—the number of years Jim had been married. Jim's mother told him that his father had left shortly after a sister was born with a birth defect that almost claimed her life and left her unable to walk. Jim's mother said his father could not endure the stress of taking care of the sister. With his father out of the picture and his mother tending almost exclusively to her weak young daughter, Jim was left to fend for himself. In addition, he felt a tremendous responsibility to help in the care of his sister and not to express any needs.

At first, Jim was not in touch with any of the childhood sadness and anger he must have experienced when left alone. As we continued our work together, he slowly began to contact these feelings, including the guilt he felt about being a healthy sibling with a sick sister. My own formulation was that, as an adult, he kept himself from being able to move in life as a way to be connected with a sister who could not walk and whom he very much wanted to save. I could understand his desperate desire to be close to people, to have somebody finally recognize and take care of him. I could also appreciate how terrifying this need was; who could blame him for once again fearing being abandoned and left to fend for himself? I also saw his isolating himself, and his own view of himself as completely helpless and hopeless, as ways to keep alive the fantasies of being rescued by both his abandoning mother and father, as well as by me.

Yet when Jim obsessed about whether or not to stay with his wife, I often felt empty and bored. It was as if he filled me with the heavy fuzziness he felt so that I could understand what it was like, so that he was not left with the entire burden himself. It was when he shared his memories of his past for the first time that I was often quite moved by his devotion to his sister, as well as his sense of being left alone and the supreme emptiness it evoked. One day he described his longing to have a father with whom he could play baseball and talk, just like the other kids. I became teary as he explained how he would hang around his friends' houses when he knew their fathers would be home, how he would pretend they were his dad. I asked if he noticed that my eyes had welled up. He said no and quickly changed the subject. On another occasion, however, he did admit to seeing me wet-eyed and said this made him very uncomfortable. He said he preferred to think of me not as another person, but as a doctor in a doctor–patient relationship.

"What if I become 'another person'?" I asked. "Then I feel pressure to have to please you and to worry about what you're thinking about me, how you're judging me," he said.

"If I'm a real person, you have to worry about taking care of me, but you also have to worry about my letting you down and not taking care of you."

The more Jim was able to identify his feelings and link them to a sense of emptiness and responsibility from his childhood, the more depressed he became. In his regression back to his painful childhood, he felt the terrible emptiness of that period, a feeling from which he had long ago dissociated. I became concerned about his growing depression and how the treatment might be contributing to it. Was he making himself hopeless so that I might find him and save him as he wished his parents would? Was he having feelings for the first time that were too much for him to bear? Did he turn against himself anger meant for his parents for not being able to save him—and toward me for making him feel the terrible emptiness? When I asked him his understanding of why he was becoming more depressed and how he felt about it, he said the following:

> I've lost the numbness, the not caring or not having a capacity to care or feel. Everything I've uncovered in here has made my emotions sharper and more recognizable. I feel them more, but I don't necessarily know how to handle them now. Before, I knew there was a part of me I didn't understand, part of me

that held back. I definitely felt I had limitations, but a part of me just accepted it and didn't really think about it. Yes, I was screwed up and not as good as I could have been, but I didn't hate life so much and struggle every day to wake up.

Now I just feel exposed. Exposed and emptied out. Now that I've unleashed everything within me, it's a big cloud, a big haze I find myself in. [He begins to cry.] The things with my sister, my father, my mother, I know too much now. I've lost my innocence, a huge part of me. I have no idea how to help myself. How can I expect anyone else to help me?

When Jim spoke like this, I began to feel the same sense of heavy hopelessness as he did. He desperately wanted to be saved but doubted he ever would be, and he was furious with me for getting his hopes up and letting him down. With equal desperation, I wanted to save him, but I was beginning to feel mostly despair myself.

In what I would retrospectively call a countertransference enactment, I began thinking of myself as the potentially loving, giving father Jim had never had. But I was filled with guilt for failing my son and not saving the day—in essence for abandoning Jim just as his father had. I also identified with his crippled sister, unable to move in any way to help him. I felt angry at Jim for putting me in this role.

Rather than stay with his despair and anger, and my own, I found myself moving away from these painful feelings by giving advice to help him get out of his depression. In addition to referring him to a psychiatrist for antidepressants, I suggested he join a basketball league. I told him to share his feelings with his wife. I suggested activities he could do, groups he could join for when he felt too depressed to get out of bed. We were both busy avoiding the relational aspect of his depression: what was happening between us that might have been causing his feelings.

Then one day I was in a particularly playful mood when I opened the door to greet Jim. I was undeterred by his dour expression and gave him a warm hello. Uncharacteristically, he smiled back at me. When he got to his chair, he noticed that there was loose change in it. The 23 cents must have slipped out of the pocket of the patient who preceded him.

"Do you want this?" Jim said, scooping up the coins and offering them to me.

"Nah," I said. "You can have it. Consider it my end-of-the-month clearance."

And then the most amazing thing happened.

Jim laughed.

Oh, it wasn't exactly a guffaw, but it was a laugh nonetheless. We had found a way in the unbearable darkness to have a moment of light.

"In all the time we've worked together, I don't think I've ever seen you laugh," I said. We had been meeting twice a week for more than a year and a half.

Jim blushed and changed the subject. Or did he? After talking about feeling more hopeful about his job (an indirect commentary on our exchange), Jim mentioned that a man had seemed to be flirting with him on the train on the way to my office. This happened to him from time to time, he said, and it always made him uncomfortable. Clearly, "some man" had been flirting with him *in* my office, too. I had not realized that I had been flirting or that he had experienced me this way. I knew I might have made him uncomfortable, as the man on the subway had. However, I was too afraid of his rejection to find a way to explore this issue. Undoubtedly, my reluctance and my own fear of rejection were greatly compounded by the fact that Jim was straight. What if he was disgusted by my advances? I was assuming that Jim thought I was straight. What if he found out I was gay? In a countertransferential way, Jim represented for me all of straight society, ready to reject me and find my sexuality repugnant.

At that moment, there were many questions I could have asked myself or possibly even of Jim. Did he wonder about my sexual orientation? How had he registered our exchange about another patient's loose change? Could he have experienced it is as an oedipal victory? What had my flirtatiousness meant to him? If it made him uncomfortable, as he seemed to be saying, then why so? And could it have really made him so uncomfortable that he was choosing to tell me about it indirectly by discussing the man on the subway? Had I detected something from Jim at the door that caused me to be flirtatious? Was I trying to break free of the quicksand-like feeling that threatened to engulf our relationship, and was Jim signaling that he was ready to do so as well? Why had I chosen today of all days? Was my decision somehow connected to our last session?

I did not, however, think of these questions, nor did I ask Jim how he had experienced me earlier in the session. Why had I missed my own participation in an erotically charged moment? Partly I think I was taken by surprise. Jim's depression seemed so deep that I had forgotten about the early stage of our work when I found him so attractive. But had that erotic charge really gone away, or was it always operating under the surface? More likely, I felt uncomfortable about having sexual feelings for a heterosexual male patient. I doubt I would have had such strong feelings of discomfort had Jim been gay. In retrospect, my guilt and anxiety about making him uneasy inhibited me from thinking "straight." But it is also possible his discomfort had to do with his excitement about being noticed rather than standing in the shadow of his sister (or my previous patient). Perhaps I could have helped him feel more alive and less depressed had I held on to those erotically charged feelings.

It was an inability to rise above the deadness that ultimately hampered this treatment. Perhaps I could have maintained a sense of excitement while also containing his despair. Perhaps I could have retained the fact that he was an attractive man who used his good looks to connect with people. Then I might have been able to hold on to the hopeful, excited, flirtatious part of Jim that was split off and needed to come alive in the treatment. Instead, my countertransferential fears about being seen as inappropriate, and of scaring Jim off, interfered with my ability to think about the palpably erotic material that was in the room, even though the patient may have been aware of it.

I believe that had Jim been gay I might have been able to recognize and tolerate the sexualized material more easily. I might have felt less afraid of being found out, of making my patient uncomfortable, and of being rejected myself. Jim felt rejected by both his parents, particularly his father. At the same time, I was afraid that Jim would reject me if we were to explore the erotic feelings, and so unconsciously I steered away. The charge that comes from erotic transference and countertransference could have moved this treatment to new and exciting places. Instead, we remained mired in a deadness that continued until the patient terminated only a short while later.

With Jim, an enactment centered on his finding 23 cents. The cost of being unaware of its meaning turned out to be far greater.

A Time to Flirt

Twenty-eight-year-old Melissa came into treatment rife with issues of rejection.

She had just been rejected by a boyfriend in a most cruel way. While she was on a two-week trip to visit her family in a Southern city, her boyfriend of four months e-mailed her that he had found another woman. He also wrote that he would appreciate Melissa's moving out of his apartment as soon as possible. It was not the first time Melissa had thrown herself into a relationship, trying desperately to please a boyfriend, only to be devastated when she found out that he did not return her interest. She had a history of falling for men who were unavailable, already involved, or unable to give her the kind of commitment she wanted.

An attractive, eager-to-please young woman, Melissa would try to gain a man's interest by flirting with him and offering herself sexually. Sometimes the man would become cold after one sexual encounter. Other times, Melissa and her love interest would begin a brief, torrid affair that would end after a period of weeks or months when the man experienced Melissa as too needy. Understandably, this rejection would leave her feeling confused and devastated.

Melissa's eagerness to find love could be traced back to her relationship with her father. A cold and dictatorial man, he ran his own company and was rarely home. When he was home, he would spend more time with his two sons, whom he was grooming to inherit the business. A man who demanded academic excellence from all his children, he spent his limited time with his only daughter criticizing her rather than playing with her. Melissa forever believed she was not good enough for her father, and she felt great pressure to succeed in school. She always hoped her father would love her if only she could find a way to please him. In this way, he was like the men she dated whom she tried so hard to please but who only ended up rejecting her.

Melissa's mother was a weak, well-meaning woman, afraid of Melissa's father and unable to calm Melissa when she worried about failing a test. Despite her anxiety about not pleasing her parents, Melissa did brilliantly in school, but her academic success never seemed enough for her father.

In the transference, I quickly became one of the men whom Melissa was going to try to please sexually in the hope of being accepted. From the beginning, she came to the sessions dressed provocatively; on a few occasions she wore a man's undershirt through which I could faintly see her nipples. Since I was aware of her sensitivity to rejection, I said nothing about this. Instead, I found myself enjoying the flirtation that took place on her way out the doorway at the end of each session. Melissa would start by making a seemingly innocuous comment about the weather or her plans for the evening, and I would jump into the brief conversation. Melissa seemed to be buffering herself against the rejection that came inevitably at the end of every session. But the way she smiled as she spoke, and the way in which I felt sexually excited, made me realize she was clearly flirting with me.

At first, I chose not to comment about Melissa's way of dressing or how we both flirted at the end of session. I knew that she was repeating a pattern with me that she had with all men, but I was unsure how to bring up the matter without shaming her. I decided it was best at this early stage to let the transference bloom and see where things went. Also, I enjoyed being a subject of her sexual interest. Flirting with her at the end of sessions was fun and exciting and, as a gay man, I felt pleased to be able to turn a woman on, and even to be turned on myself.

Then, only a few months into treatment, Melissa brought in a dream:

> I'm on an airplane that's about to take me home to visit my parents. I'm afraid of flying and particularly nervous about this flight. I'm sitting there, feeling alone and frightened, when my boss gets on the plane and sits down next to me. I think, "Oh, great, this is the last thing I need. I'll have to make small talk with him all the way to [the city where she was going]. But then the strangest thing happened. Rather than being cool and critical, as my boss really is, the man in the dream was quite warm and he began to talk to me. When I told him I was nervous about flying, he calmed me down by telling me how safe it was to fly. It was nice to have a man's attention that way, and I remember relaxing and feeling good about the flight.

Melissa's associations went immediately to her boss. She repeated how surprised she was that he could have the effect of calming her down when in real life he just made her more nervous. Perhaps the boss in her dream was really her father, she thought.

"Could I be the man in your dream?" I asked. "You've sometimes described me as distant and told me how that makes you feel nervous."

"Oh no, you couldn't be my boss in the dream," she said. "I remember now. In the dream, my boss and I get off the plane before it takes off, find some private place in the lounge, and have sex. So, of course, it couldn't be you."

Nervously I asked, "Why do you say of course it couldn't be me?"

Melissa blushed. "I wouldn't dream of having sex with you. You're my therapist."

"Does that mean you can't have a fantasy about me? After all, we talked about the way you sometimes engage sexually with men and then feel rejected. Why wouldn't that issue come up here as well? In fact, I've noticed we seem to make small talk together at the end of sessions in a way that feels almost flirtatious."

Although I was concerned about making this comment, I decided to do so because Melissa's dream could be reasonably interpreted as her having erotic feelings toward me.

"Are you saying you're flirting with me?" she demanded to know.

Here was the question I dreaded. But at least we could have the issue of erotic feelings on the table now. I gulped and continued, "It feels a little as though we are flirting with each other, no?"

"No!" Melissa said emphatically. "It doesn't feel that way at all."

"You make it sound as if it would be terrible if it were true."

"Well, you're my therapist. We're not supposed to have those feelings for each other."

"Actually, we are not supposed to act on those feelings here. We most certainly can have them, however."

Melissa was silent for a moment. When she spoke, she looked at the floor rather than at me. "Well, I guess it's possible I'm flirting with you. I have to admit I like to flirt. It makes me feel attractive and wanted."

"Especially if the man flirts back," I said.

Melissa looked up at me and smiled. "Yes, especially then." I was relieved that my hunch about our mutual flirting had been correct and that my mentioning it had not scared off Melissa, but rather had opened something up in the treatment.

In the weeks that followed, Melissa dressed as she always had—some days more provocatively than others—and we both continued our flirtation at the door. She began to speak more about her fear that, like her father, I would put demands on her and disappoint or abandon her. It was the first time she spoke about me in the treatment.

At the time I started treating Melissa, I was a candidate in analytic training, without a private office and using my home phone number for patients to contact me. One Sunday afternoon I received a phone call from Melissa while I was reading for a class.

"Hello Eric?" she said in a friendly tone. "It's Melissa. I have two tickets to the ballet tonight that I just found out I won't be able to use. So I'm calling people I know to see if they would like them. Do you have any interest?"

My plans for the evening included reheating dinner and reading for the class. I was smart enough, though, to thank her but tell her I did, in fact, have plans. I had mixed feelings about her phone call. I was both touched and put off by her familiarity. I realized that Melissa's transference had grown. Yet I also had to admit that, when she said she had two tickets to the ballet, I had an immediate fantasy that she was going to ask me to be her date. In my fantasy, I would have said yes.

At our next session, I asked Melissa what it was like to call me at home and offer me the ballet tickets in what seemed like a very personal gesture.

"I knew you were going to ask that," she said. "I was unsure whether I should call you, but I had these tickets and it seemed a shame to let them go to waste. I didn't mean anything more by the phone call than that. Can't a cigar be just a cigar?"

"Not when it's a penis," I thought. I shared my fantasy that I momentarily had thought she was going to ask me out on a date. To my shock and dismay, Melissa burst into tears.

"Why must you see everything I do as devious and sexual?" she cried. "I thought I was doing a nice thing."

I felt horrible but continued. "It *was* a nice thing," I said. "But when you consider that you were calling me at my home over the weekend to see if I wanted tickets to a social event . . . well, it's not the kind of thing that normally happens between us."

My comment only made Melissa cry more. "Why are you poking at me?" she said between sobs.

It was then that I realized that I was feeling stupid and awkward with Melissa, as she felt with her father. I was open to this projective identification because this was also how I had felt many times with my own father.

When Melissa stopped crying, I told her that it was not my intention to poke her, but rather to understand what was happening between us. My sharing my fantasy seemed to have caused a very strong reaction. There was nothing at all wrong with this reaction, but since it was so strong, I wanted to understand it.

Melissa was unable to say anything more than that she was unsure what had happened that had been so upsetting for her. I asked if she remembered what upset her, and she said, "Something about your thinking I was asking you out for a date."

"What was upsetting about that?"

"Because it makes it seem like I had some ulterior motive. I would never ask you on a date. You're my therapist."

I told Melissa that I was reminded of the time she was sure I was not her boss in the dream, because, I being her therapist, we would never have sex. "You were not asking me out, and I knew that—I said it was my fantasy. It's completely understandable that either of us can have a fantasy about being romantically involved."

Melissa remained flustered despite my assurances, and the rest of the session was tense. As a result, the erotic transference and counter-transference ebbed.

Perhaps because I missed our flirtatious good-byes, several months later I made an unexpectedly intimate phone call, although it did not quite start out that way. I needed to call Melissa to see if we could meet at a different time for one of our sessions that week. I called after 10 o'clock in the morning and was surprised to hear grogginess in her voice, as if I had just awakened her. (Melissa worked from home, and I assumed she would have been at her desk for some time.)

"Did I wake you?" I asked without introducing myself. I was surprised by the tone of informality in my voice. I sounded like a lover calling the morning after. I made a note to explore Melissa's feelings in the next session.

As it turned out, I would not have to bring up the subject myself. Melissa, who by now was lying on the couch, reported the following dream:

> We were having a session, only instead of lying on the couch I was lying in a bed. I was absorbed in what I was saying and I wasn't looking at you. I looked up at you and you smiled. It was a relaxed smile, like a façade cracking. I smiled back and thought, "I don't think I've ever seen Eric smile so warmly before." I had a feeling of being seen and appreciated. We had a special moment of connection. And then you got into bed with me. At first I felt uncomfortable, as though you were doing something wrong. But after a moment or two it felt right.

Considering that Melissa had been denying any possibility of erotic feelings, I was surprised she was able to tell me this dream. Her associations were that she had been finding herself feeling close to me recently, and, although this new closeness was unnerving, it also made her feel good. She remained concerned that she would become too dependent on me and that I would let her down, but more and more she was feeling confident about being with me and about the work we were doing.

I said I found it interesting that she had had a dream about me getting into bed with her right after my telephone call, and I wondered how she had experienced the call. She said that at first it unnerved her, because I sounded so informal. But then she felt good about it. It was as if we were friends, and she liked the intimate tone.

Shortly after my phone call, Melissa began dating a man named Roger. This was her first date in a while, and she was being careful not to rush into things. Instead of describing him as exciting, sexy, and dangerous, she used words like sturdy, smart, interesting, and considerate. After several weeks of casual dating, Melissa began to feel this could be a serious relationship, and she decided to sleep with Roger. My sense was that our erotic enactment had enabled her to feel good about herself sexually and to feel confident that she could get to know another kind of considerate man without having to be let down by him.

Nine months later, Melissa announced her engagement to Roger. Shortly after the wedding, she became pregnant with twins. As she planned to become a mother, I noticed that the erotic feelings in the treatment seemed to dissipate and were replaced by mutual admiration. Before she gave birth, Melissa said she wanted to end therapy for she felt she had gained everything she had hoped for from the treatment. She was happily married and was soon to become a mother, and she no longer worried so much as she got close to people that they would abandon her. I agreed that it was time to end, and we set a termination date just before her due date, with the understanding that we would meet one more time after she gave birth so I could see the babies and see how she was doing. We did, in fact, have one final session in which I got to see her son and daughter, both of whom looked just like mom.

Why was I able to feel comfortable with my erotic feelings toward Melissa, although I had phobically avoided them with Jim? I think one big difference was their genders. I believe it is more permissible for me to have erotic feelings toward a woman than toward a straight man since my own fear of rejection is much less with a woman. The idea of coming on to a straight man seems dangerous, since he may react with discomfort or even disdain. Yet a straight woman, even one who knows my sexual orientation, presumably would be less likely to feel uncomfortable, which is not unexpected in the "normal" heterosexual dyad. Even when she does feel uncomfortable, as Melissa did, I am less likely to feel as if I were doing something wrong by having sexual feelings for a woman rather than for a straight man.

Nonetheless, it is interesting to note that, even with Melissa, the erotic transference and countertransference were less intense than with some gay patients with whom I have worked (see, e.g., chapter 8). I believe that I feel most comfortable having strong sexual feelings for a gay man, since this is closest to my everyday experience, and I do not have to feel that I have to hide my sexual orientation.

My work with Jim and Melissa illustrates how the erotic transference and countertransference between a gay therapist and a straight patient can be as complex and varied as in any other dyad. Although the exact nature of the transference–countertransference will vary depending on the analyst's sexual orientation—as well as each member of the dyad's personality and organizing principles—there is no less a multiplicity of feelings and reactions, from deadness to erotic excitement, than when the patient and the analyst have the same sexual orientation.

Interestingly, in both cases the sexual transference–countertransference started at the very beginning of treatment, only to resurface with my joking about the loose change (in the case of Jim) or continue for several years (in the case of Melissa). In both cases, the erotic feelings enlivened the work (even if only temporarily with Jim), proving that erotic countertransference can be an area of creativity and growth, even if it is also fraught with uncertainty.

6

AND BABY MAKES THREE
Living a Fantasy with a
Heterosexual Mother

When I opened the door for my new 1:15 patient, I was not prepared
for what I saw. Standing before me was a petite woman in her ninth
month of pregnancy. Deborah was tremendous, and slightly un-
gainly. She lumbered into my office and lowered herself to a seated
position on the couch.

"I guess I didn't tell you over the phone that I was pregnant," she
said, undoubtedly noticing the look of surprise on my face. "This will
be my first."

"Mine too," I thought. In the short time I had been an analyst I
had never worked with a pregnant woman. I was already thinking of
the logistics involved in making a quick connection with someone
who might be taking some time off to have her baby within weeks of
our beginning and who might not return at all. (Deborah had seemed
particularly nervous in our brief conversation over the phone.) I also

73

wondered what she would do with the baby during our sessions. Would I have a squirming infant in my office for the first week (or weeks) of the sessions after the birth? That could enable an early bonding experience between me and the patient. But having a screaming, pooping, distracting baby in the room could also be a disaster.

Having arranged herself as comfortably as she could on the couch, Deborah began to tell me her story. She was feeling depressed, she said, partly because of all the changes in her life. Twenty-nine years old, she had just moved to the area with her husband, Dave, who had been reassigned to New York from his company's office in the Midwest. Deborah had quit her job on the fast track of a successful Fortune 500 company in order to be with Dave. Although she had mixed feelings, she and Dave had decided that she would not work for a while and instead would stay home and take care of the baby.

"We think it's best for the baby to have a mother around rather than to be raised by a nanny," she said. The way she said "we" made me wonder how much of this decision was her husband's, how much Deborah might be afraid of looking for work in New York, how much her own desires to be with her baby might be projected onto her husband, and what their relationship was like. As she continued, it became clear that she was deeply ambivalent about being a mother. "This wasn't planned," she said, touching her stomach. "I really don't know if I'm ready to be a mother. I've read probably a dozen books on parenting and I'm afraid of the responsibility. I'm afraid I'll make a mistake."

For Deborah, making a mistake was the worst thing in the world. She had a great need to be perfect, and, as a result, when she accomplished anything, it did not feel like much of an accomplishment. I looked at her stomach and realized how difficult being a mother—good enough, but by necessity imperfect—would be for her.

Being a patient was difficult enough. Deborah said she was deeply ashamed of needing therapy, and she worried about what other people would think if they knew she was in treatment. Although she had been in therapy once before for six months, she had not liked the woman therapist, who she said had remained mostly silent. Deborah had quit that treatment suddenly. She was motivated to seek treatment again, despite her great reluctance, because of problems in her marriage. Dave, successful in a competitive field, worked long hours and paid little attention to her. When he was around the house, he was consumed with his own interests—preparing for work, watching TV—rather than spending time with Deborah. He rarely inquired about how she was, what was going on in her life, or what she might desire from him. When she confronted him, he responded with how hard he worked and that he needed whatever free time he had to relax on his own. According to Deborah, he denied they had a problem and refused to enter couples therapy.

In addition to marital problems, Deborah was homesick for the Midwest and wished to be near her friends and family. After living here for several months, she was having trouble adjusting to the fast pace of New York. She missed working and the power that came with her former position. She seemed to gain a sense of self solely from her work accomplishments. I was getting a clear picture of a narcissistically vulnerable woman craving to be noticed, yet afraid of what others would think of her needs and dependencies—hence her fears about therapy. I could appreciate how difficult it must be for her to go from being a high-powered businesswoman to a stay-at-home, expectant mom in a strange, unfriendly city.

Deborah reported that her own mother had been quite distant and critical. Deborah had always felt that no matter what she did, it was never good enough for her mother. As a child, she yearned for her mother to be more attentive, but the older woman seemed largely uninterested. Her mom sounded quite a bit like her husband, I said, and Deborah seemed impressed by this insight. "It's true," she said. "I never thought about that." I could sense Deborah's mistrust of me begin to melt a little. Now that she was pregnant, she vowed not to make the same mistakes as her mother had with her but was terrified she would not be a good-enough parent herself.

When I asked about Deborah's father, her face glowed. "My daddy meant the world to me," she said. "When I was a little girl he was a radio engineer and he would take me to work with him, and I got to play with all the microphones and buttons and dials when no show was on the air." She obviously idealized her father, whose attentiveness partly made up for her mother's lack of interest. The all-good father and the witchlike mother—the sides were starkly drawn. Unfortunately, Deborah's father died of a heart attack when she was eight years old. Although Deborah was devastated, her stern mother would not allow her to go to the funeral or mourn in any way. "After the first week, she would yell at me for crying," Deborah said. Within a year, her mother had met and married another man whom Deborah resented for taking her beloved father's place.

I had a sense in the first session that Deborah begrudgingly liked me, and I liked her immediately for her spunk and sense of humor. With the attentive comments I made, she apparently saw in me the loving approval of her father. I also think I represented the "good-enough" mother (Winnicott, 1951) for whom she had always longed. I knew, however, that I could quickly become the bad mother/stepfather. Furthermore, from the way she answered some of my questions, I could see that behind her spunk was a real prickliness for which I would have to be prepared.

As we agreed to work together, the question of Deborah's pregnancy came to the fore. She told me that she would like to take a week or two off after giving birth, and then she asked if it would be all right to bring her baby for the first few sessions until she could find a sitter. Her request certainly seemed fair, but it left me with mixed feelings. The rational side of me knew it would give me an important opportunity to bond with her, win her trust, and see directly what kind of mother she was. I would have the opportunity to coo over the baby and win valuable brownie points.

Yet many possibilities made me nervous. What if the baby spent 45 minutes crying, disturbing my suitemates, making therapy difficult, and making both of us feel helpless? As a gay man with no parenting experience, I was out of my element. What did I know about taking care of a baby? I had never held an infant. What if Deborah offered me the chance? I would prove my ignorance and reveal my lack of experience as a father. Would questions follow about whether I was married or gay? What if she wanted parenting advice? And what would I do if she breast fed during a session?

Although I was nervous about the idea of having a crying infant in the office, I knew it would be a mistake to say no. Deborah would certainly not stay in treatment unless I agreed to this arrangement.

And so we began our work. A few weeks later, I got a call from Deborah to say she had given birth to a six-pound, eight-ounce baby named Nicole. She was calling me from the hospital, partly to give me as much notice as possible before canceling our next once-weekly appointment; but also I was already becoming an important person in her life, and she was obviously so excited about sharing her good news with me that she could not wait until she got home.

As we had agreed, Deborah said she wanted to take two weeks off but would return at the end of the month with Nicole, "if that was still okay." I told her that, of course, it was, congratulated her, and inquired about how she and the baby were doing. I could practically see her beam over the telephone at my interest.

When Deborah returned for her next meeting, she arrived with a bouncer seat and her newborn daughter. After what seemed like a proper amount of time admiring the baby, I returned to my seat. Much to my relief, Nicole was incredibly well behaved throughout the session; she stirred from her sleep only once or twice. Deborah was easily able to rock her back to sleep with her foot practically without being distracted. "See," I told myself, "this won't be too bad for a few weeks until she can find someone to watch the baby."

And so the collusion began. For the first few weeks, Deborah talked about her painful childhood and the challenges of being a new mother as Nicole slept through most of the session. My anxiety that Deborah would ask me for parenting advice—advice that I, a then single gay man without a child, would not be able to give—proved unwarranted. Actually my nervousness kept me from wondering why she was *not* asking for advice, or why she was not curious to know if I was a parent. She may have not wanted to risk that I would become deidealized if the answers to her questions were disappointing.

Deborah said she was making no headway in finding a sitter. She did not want to trust her daughter to a stranger, and she had yet to befriend any other new mothers who might give a recommendation. But, as the weeks dragged on, I soon realized that these were just excuses and that Deborah had mixed feelings about finding a sitter. She worried that something would happen if her daughter were away from her careful watch and then she would be blamed as an unfit mother. I theorized that she also used Nicole as a living receptacle for her projected feelings of adequacy; she considered herself flawed, yet Nicole was the perfect little well-behaved baby she could both show off and try to experience as a part of herself. Also, she clearly liked bringing Nicole to session. My assumption was that Nicole's presence made it safer for Deborah to be in therapy with me; she was a ready distraction in case things became too close and uncomfortable. And as long as she came to session, I was able to see Deborah as a loving mother, rather than the prickly person of whom I had had a glimpse in the first session. I was beginning to notice that Deborah would suddenly turn her attention to Nicole when I asked her a difficult question she might wish to avoid or when her annoyance might have erupted.

When I wondered aloud what it would be like for just the two of us to be in the room together, without the baby, Deborah began to rock Nicole with her foot even though Nicole was not stirring. "It would be fine," she said defensively. "I just can't bear to leave Nicole with a stranger. You hear so many horror stories."

"Maybe Nicole's presence here makes you more comfortable," I said. "It ensures that nothing dangerous will come up here."

Even given such a provocative interpretation, Deborah seemed completely uninterested, a sign to me that she was defending against something. "No," she said. "Like I said, I just can't find a sitter. But I promise I will by next week."

I let the subject go at that, and for several more weeks Deborah continued to bring Nicole. I continued to discuss with her what I thought were some of the meanings of bringing her daughter. We also talked about practical ways to find a sitter and what seemed to make that difficult. I attempted to connect this difficulty to her feeling of having been left alone as a child, particularly after her father's death. However, most attempts to explore analytically what might be happening went only so far and led to no changes in her behavior.

Soon the weeks became months, and Deborah continued to bring her baby to sessions. During this period, some good, even deep, work was done, even with Nicole's presence and Deborah's defensiveness. I became the first person to whom she admitted having been fondled as a child by a friend of the family. We explored her childhood further and connected it to the theme that, if she was not perfect she was unlovable and that this perspective left her feeling hurt and angry. She wanted to feel special, yet with her parents and her husband she felt anything but unique. Deborah complained about Dave and his inattentiveness and long hours at work. In the transference, I had become the good husband and father of Deborah's baby, no doubt another reason she continued to bring Nicole to session. At the beginning of one hour, she held Nicole up and said, "Say hello to Eric. Can you say Eric? He's the man you see more than your . . . well, he's one of the three people you see the most."

Deborah was not the only one enjoying such a fantasy. This single gay man now had his own wife and child—an instant family and the fulfillment of a lifelong wish. I found myself comparing Nicole with other children. Nicole is better behaved than that boy. Nicole is smarter than that girl. I had accepted the fact that I would never have a traditional heterosexual marriage and had too many reservations as a gay man about becoming a father. But there was still a part of me that did not accept this state of affairs and longed for the fantasy of living the heterosexual dream: a wife, kids, and a house in the suburbs with a picket fence. I liked the idea of having an instant family; I was now doing something that would please both my distant and critical father and my Jewish mother, who yearned to be a grandmother. I also liked winning a competition with Deborah's real husband to see who was more loving and attentive.

The countertransferential idea of a cozy marriage to Deborah was so appealing that I found it difficult to set a boundary with her about how long she could continue to bring Nicole. My attempts to analyze Deborah's resistance, and for her to look at her dreams and wishes in bringing Nicole, seemed fake and halfhearted. Frankly, I wanted Nicole there almost as much as Deborah did. I did not think about it at the time, but I had yet to see Deborah's prickly side. On some level I may have realized that Nicole's presence was protecting me from it.

Then matters went from bad to worse. One cold winter's day, Deborah arrived early while I was out to lunch with a colleague. Lately, she had taken to coming 10 minutes early or so, eager to see me and continue our fantasy romance. Nonetheless, Deborah was not interested in attending more than once a week; she said she was afraid doing so would make her into a Woody Allen–like New York cliché. And then what would people think? I also believe she was afraid of dependency and of pushing the fantasy of our blissful marriage too far to where it might lose its magic.

On this brisk afternoon, she had been already waiting outside for 10 minutes when I returned 10 minutes before session and let her into the waiting room. She and Nicole were both cold and cranky. Feeling guilty, I began the session almost immediately and even apologized for keeping them waiting out in the cold. The next week I made sure I was in my office at least 20 minutes early just in case. (Deborah went back to being her usual 10 minutes early.) My vision was so clouded by a desire to please her that I was avoiding seeing any other sides to my beloved Deborah, including her anger. I was so eager to be the good husband and father that I was unable to see her as anything but the perfect mother and wife—exactly as she wanted to be seen.

On another occasion, seven months after Nicole's birth, Deborah came in very excited. She took Nicole out of the stroller, placed her on the floor, and exclaimed, "Look what she's learned to do!" Nicole obediently began rolling slightly on the floor. I voiced my approval, although the idea of a mobile baby capable of knocking things over made me uncomfortable. After Nicole rolled around a little longer, Deborah picked her up and noticed that she had dirt from my carpet on her jumpsuit. Deborah looked me straight in the eye. "Your carpet must be dirty," she said. It was obvious from the look on her face that she expected my carpet to be vacuumed next time for "our" daughter.

The next week I obediently pulled out the vacuum cleaner and cleaned the carpet so that Nicole would not get dirty. When I felt disappointed that Deborah did not notice, I realized for the first time how much the transference and countertransference were dovetailing. Deborah felt disappointed whenever she did anything to please people that went unnoticed, and now I was feeling exactly the same way. I knew that I was deeply engaged in an enactment and that I needed to do something to address it directly. I decided it was time to confront Deborah and tell her that she had to stop bringing Nicole, even though I was hesitant to ruin the Deborah–Eric mutual admiration society or make her angry and reveal sides of herself I might not want to see. And I knew I would miss Nicole. I felt like a man who was divorcing and would not have visitation rights. I would be returning to being a single gay man again.

The next week, I began the session by telling Deborah I had been thinking a lot about her still bringing Nicole to sessions. Our agreement had been that Nicole would come for a few weeks until Deborah found someone to babysit her. It had now been seven months. I was curious to know why both of us were so comfortable with this new arrangement, what we were both hoping for and avoiding. Deborah gave the same answer she had always given: that she just had not been able to find a babysitter whom she could trust. I said I found that hard to believe. "Nicole can be a convenient distraction from the two of us being alone and looking at vulnerable issues together," I said. "And I also wonder if we both aren't sharing a fantasy that I am Nicole's father, since I know you have many complaints about Dave's lack of involvement with the baby."

Although I had voiced before the issue of Nicole as a distraction, this was the first time I had brought up the idea that we were both sharing a connubial fantasy. I chose to include myself in the interpretation for several reasons. First, I hoped it would diminish any blame Deborah might feel, for she was vulnerable to narcissistic injury. I also felt it important to try to open up an analytic space, one in which Deborah could wonder about my participation and be more curious about herself and her own motivations. I knew she must have had feelings and fantasies all along about my reaction to her bringing Nicole to session, even though every attempt to look at them had failed. Finally, I think I made the "we" statement as a way for me to start to break out of my role in the enactment.

Deborah did not share in my "act of freedom" (Symington, 1983), but instead blushed and squirmed. For a moment she said nothing. My comment about the two of us being in the room alone together and about my sharing her fantasy may have been too erotically charged for her. She might have heard me saying that I wanted the two of us to be alone so that something sexual would happen. This may have, in fact, been her fantasy.

"I don't know what you mean," she said. "I just haven't been able to find someone to take care of Nicole. I will by next week, I promise."

I knew that Deborah might be experiencing me now as her critical mother. To be frank, I was a little annoyed with her stubbornness and her inability to look at the analytic issues. She had promised to find a babysitter "by next week" on several occasions. I was also angry at myself for my role in the enactment. So I pushed ahead, the tone of annoyance possibly evident in my voice.

"You've made that promise before but have been unable to keep it," I said. "I know it's difficult, but it's been seven months since we've met without Nicole. I think it would be important for us to be able to do that."

Deborah looked annoyed and then hissed, "I said I'd do it." When I attempted to explore her anger at me, she claimed she was not angry and switched the subject.

The next week, Deborah arrived alone, and more elegantly dressed than usual. When I greeted her at the door, she smiled coyly and walked to the couch.

"See, I'm a woman of my word. I said I would leave Nicole home and I did. Aren't you proud of me?"

Deborah had left one child home and brought another—herself, a little girl yearning for my approval. As a matter of fact, I *was* proud of her, but I hesitated to say so. I did not know if telling her I was proud would close down her anger from the previous session. Rather than get trapped into saying whether I was proud or not, I tried a middle ground.

"Aaah, you left Nicole home," I said. "What was that like for you?"

Deborah look devastated by my cool response. "That's all you're going to say? I thought you'd be proud of me."

If my goal was to arouse Deborah's anger, I certainly succeeded. Deborah became icy and withdrawn. She said nothing for some time.

"I can see that you're angry with me," I said.

"I'm not angry," she said. "I'm annoyed. I just thought you'd be proud of me."

In retrospect, this would have been the perfect time to explore Deborah's disappointment and how it left her feeling hurt and angry. This was a common theme in her life. But, rather than explore how my measured response had left her angry, I felt guilty about hurting her and decided to backtrack and give her the affirmation she had been seeking.

"Yes, of course I'm proud of you. It must not have been an easy thing to do."

"No, it wasn't." She crossed her arms angrily, sat way back on the couch, and refused to say another word. Saying I was proud of her after she had prodded me a second time was too little too late as far as she was concerned, and now I would have to pay.

"Deborah, I can see that you are angry at me. Can you tell me about it."

"I'm not angry at you."

"You *sound* angry at me. I think you're angry because I didn't say I was proud of you soon enough."

"I'm not angry, I'm annoyed."

"Okay, tell me how you're annoyed."

"You already said why yourself."

I had mixed feelings about what seemed to be a petulant child sitting across from me. On one hand, I was glad to see Deborah's anger. Any time a patient shows previously suppressed emotions, it is an important moment in the treatment. I hypothesized that my sudden coolness must have reenacted both her mother's indifference and the sudden death of her idealized father, and she must have pulled away with anger and shame. But Deborah's newly emergent angry self seemed difficult and unpleasant. I longingly wondered what happened to the Deborah who I fantasized was my wife and mother of our child? What happened to the good Deborah, who enjoyed seeing me and whom I enjoyed seeing? I did not like this new Deborah, who remained sullen throughout the session. She had become the punishing mother to me, and I had a new understanding of what childhood must been like for her. I suddenly had a new appreciation for her husband—my former rival—who no doubt frequently was on the receiving end of this anger and sullenness.

I also had a better idea of what Nicole's presence had been helping us avoid. Just as I had thought, it was Deborah's anger. Something must have been frightening about this anger, which she now was both showing to me and trying to deny at the same time. I said this to Deborah, who, without softening, replied, "If I showed you my anger, it would be too much for you."

"How so?"

"It just would be," she said. "When I get angry it spills out all over the place. It's ugly. Dave pulls away and says he won't speak with me when I'm angry."

"Are you afraid that if you're angry here I'll pull away?" I asked.

Deborah shrugged her shoulders and remained silent.

"I think that must be the case," I said. "Your anger must feel pretty strong."

"It doesn't feel pretty strong. It *is* pretty strong."

"Tell me about it."

"What's to tell? I yell and scream and sometimes I throw things."

"Do you feel like throwing something at me?" I asked.

"I said I was annoyed at you. I'm not angry."

And so went the next few sessions. Each time Deborah would arrive without Nicole but with a chip on her shoulder. She would begin each session by sitting down, crossing her arms, and saying she almost did not come in that day. I was beginning to worry that she might end the treatment. I felt powerless, hopeless, and angry. But then I became aware of another feeling, one I had not recognized before: grief. I felt terribly sad. Clearly, I had not mourned the loss of Nicole and of my fantasy. However, I also needed to mourn the loss of the old Deborah, whose love for me seemed unequivocal—until it vanished so quickly. All this made me think of how an eight-year-old Deborah had been prohibited from mourning her father's death.

The next time we met, I said to Deborah, "I think you feel you've lost something special here. This leaves you feeling depressed, confused, and hopeless, as when your father died. I think you're wondering why I don't love you anymore."

Deborah began to cry. "When you didn't say you were proud of me, I couldn't believe it," she sobbed. "I was sure you'd be proud of me. That's all I kept thinking on the cab ride over here. And when you weren't, I didn't know what to do." Deborah covered her eyes as she cried.

I told Deborah that I could appreciate her feeling hurt, ashamed, and confused. A special feeling she had had here was gone and that loss left her feeling humiliated for having enjoyed it.

"Maybe I was wrong to have felt it," she said.

"What could be wrong with feeling special?" I asked. "It's too bad you can't feel more of that way toward yourself. You don't need to be the perfect mother to be okay with yourself. You need to tolerate the different parts of your personality, including the side that wants to be affirmed and the side that gets hurt and angry when you're not."

The enactment around Nicole was at the core of what we needed to work on: Deborah's conflicts about her anger and her avoidance of it by idealization. I contributed to the enactment by avoiding my conflicts about being gay as I worked hard to be an idealizable "heterosexual" husband and father. It was only when I stopped being the "perfect" father and husband that Deborah's prickliness could emerge in full force. I do not know if the fantasy I had with Deborah would have been as strong if I were a straight single man, a straight married man with children, or a partnered gay man with children for that matter. I doubt it. I believe the dynamic of Deborah's using Nicole and her idealization of me to avoid her prickliness would have been present at any rate.

Maybe one day my partner and I will change our minds and have a child. Even then, I will have to mourn the loss of the "perfect" heterosexual life. In the meantime, at least I will always have memories of Nicole.

7

THE ANALYST FALLS ASLEEP
Longing, Resistance, and the Dread of
Desire in a Gay Analytic Dyad

Of all the clinical moments in my work with 48-year-old Steve, perhaps the one that best epitomizes the treatment occurred at the end of our first year together.

I fell asleep.

Not just a few seconds' nod that Steve, lying on the couch, might not have noticed. But a slumber of several minutes at the end of the session that was impossible to miss.

Mind you, I am not in the habit of taking naps during my sessions. This is the only time I have ever fallen asleep on a patient. And although I can joke about it now, I was quite embarrassed when it happened, and I took this occurrence very seriously.

I was curious about so many things. Why had I fallen asleep at this point in the treatment? What did it mean that I was dead to the world in a treatment that often had a sense of deadness? What had Steve done while I was slumbering? What was he feeling about what had happened, and how would this affect our work together?

The session had started off uneventfully enough. I was listening to Steve talk about some aspect of his job as an investment analyst when my mind began to drift. The next thing I knew I heard a familiar voice from the couch.

"Eric," he said quietly. I opened my eyes and saw that Steve was sitting up now and looking at me. "Eric, the session is over and I have to go to work."

Even in my groggy, humiliated state, I realized the irony of my patient's telling me we had to end the session, rather than the other way around. He was trying to take care of me in this terribly awkward moment. "Dear God! Did I fall asleep?" I asked. Steve nodded, looking as embarrassed as I was.

"I asked you a question and you didn't answer," he said. "So I looked around and I could see that you were asleep."

"Oh, God!" I said. "Steve, I'm so sorry."

"Up late watching the playoff game?" he asked.

I was aware he was offering me an excuse that might save face for both of us. It was also an excuse that was more likely to locate me as a straight man, or at least as the kind of gay man who liked team sports—that is, a gay man like Steve. He had already made it clear that he did not want to know my sexual orientation. In fact, he wished to know as little about me as possible.

"Let's talk about what happened next time," I suggested.

I was wide awake now, and my mind was certainly alert. I knew from our history together, and from his comments about the playoff game, that he would try to explain away what had happened rather than talk about how it felt to have me fall asleep. I looked forward to the next session with anticipation and dread. It would not be easy for either of us to talk about the enactment.

Steve began our next session as if it were any other. As was his custom, he arrived 10 minutes late. He lay down on the couch and stared silently into space. I realized that he was not spontaneously going to address what had happened in the last session.

"Were you not going to talk about my falling asleep?" I asked.

"That was my plan," he said.

"Why is that?" I asked.

"Because I didn't want to make you feel uncomfortable. I didn't want you to feel guilty or anything like that. It was no big deal."

I told Steve that I thought it was a big deal but that I realized he might be uncomfortable talking about it. I asked him to tell me more about my feeling guilty, and also how he felt about what had happened. Was he angry with me? Worried about me? Maybe he thought I found him boring, as many patients would have done under the circumstances.

Steve said he did not think that was the case, nor was he angry with me. He simply assumed that I had not gotten enough sleep the night before. He remembered hoping that a truck would pass by the window, loud enough to wake me up so we could continue the session as if nothing had happened. "After all, it's not like this is the fourth or fifth time you've fallen asleep. Then I might be mad."

"It's nice to know I have three or four more naps coming," I quipped.

Steve's need to protect me came as no surprise. The incident reminded me of how sensitive he himself was to embarrassment. He was trying to save me the humiliation he so easily felt and might be feeling now if he thought about why I fell asleep.

When I asked Steve what he had done while I slept, he told me that he had continued the session silently, in his own mind. He said he actually preferred doing that since he did not have to interact with me and worry about how I would respond. He said he did not remember the content of his silent session, but that he had continued along the lines of what he had been talking about to me when he presumed I was awake.

Even though I already knew Steve needed to keep me at a distance, I still was struck by how little my presence seemed to matter to him—or, quite the opposite, how anxious it made him. I asked him what response he was worried I would have if he interacted with me, and he said there was nothing specific—just that I would be forming an opinion about him. My being awake and attentive to him carried the danger of my having thoughts about him and arousing feelings within each of us—need, dependency, desire, even sexual longings—and these feelings were very dangerous. I wondered if my falling asleep was a result of Steve's having intolerable feelings of closeness that he would not have wanted either of us to know about. I was aware that early on in the treatment I had had strong romantic and sexual feelings for Steve. Recently, however, they had diminished when he stopped talking about his sexual fantasies and instead concentrated on everyday work issues.

In five years together, I have grown used to Steve's wrapping himself in a cocoon of safety, neither letting in nor showing need or desire. Living a life that is utterly alone, he works long hours and has only a handful of friends. At 48, he is still a virgin. He made two attempts in college to have sex with women but was unable to have an erection. He has never been with a man, but his fantasies—to the degree he lets himself fantasize—are exclusively about other men. He thinks of himself as gay. But other than to me, he has come out only to one other person, a close woman friend. He has no gay friends and no intention of acting on his sexuality. He is ashamed of being gay and regards his sexuality as an alien, disturbing part of himself best dealt with through dissociation.

Even in the treatment, he allows himself to feel no desire, at least not outwardly. I have suggested he come more frequently than twice a week, hoping this would give us a chance to work in the transference on his fears and vulnerabilities. He says that increasing the frequency would be outside his comfort level. He is unable to articulate exactly what would make him uncomfortable. My own sense is that, by coming three times a week, he might have to deal with his sexuality, reveal more of himself than he wants to, and experience an intensification of his feelings toward me.

The same holds true for a full 45-minute session. Steve is always 10 to 15 minutes late. We have talked about his lateness many times. Well, I have talked about it. Steve mostly sidesteps the issue.

I have always been conflicted about how to handle Steve's lateness. Do I press him to come on time? Or do I continue to explore what makes him want to shorten the sessions? He says he is simply late for everything. No offense. But I often do take offense. At least I did at the beginning. By no longer trying to analyze his lateness, I consciously believe I accept the conditions he has set for having a relationship, however attenuated, with me. I worry, though, that I have gotten so used to his being late that I take it for granted, even look forward to it. At other times, I pelt him with questions:

What does *he* think it means that he is always late?

Is he expressing anger or aggression?

Is he testing to see if I can tolerate his lateness; to see if he is important enough or special enough to wait for?

How does he think I feel while waiting for him?

What does he think I do in the time that he is not here?

What would it be like to spend the full 45 minutes with me? What is he afraid would happen if he did?

How would he like me to respond to his perpetual lateness?

I have confronted him and suggested that, if he really wants to get work done, he should come on time. I have wondered out loud what we may be enacting from his past. I have thought about how coming late puts him more in charge—he decides when the session will start—and this may seem to him more safe. I have been angry, empathic, apathetic. And still he comes late. Yet he comes.

Not surprisingly, Steve is afraid of what will happen if he talks *too much* about being gay. Doing so might lead him to the slippery slope of acting on his feelings. He is afraid he will have to tell his younger sister and, worse yet, his parents. To do so would fill him and them with shame and self-blame—exactly what he feared I would feel if he had chastised me for falling asleep. I believe that, in addition to his being ashamed of his sexuality, there are parts of Steve that he is afraid

to show to his family and me, particularly his aggression and assertiveness. My goal is to help Steve incorporate the dissociated aspects of himself, even if that means he chooses to stay in the closet
as a gay man.

There is, of course, no way for me to know how Steve's parents
would react if he were ever to come out to them. Steve rarely speaks
about his parents in treatment. If I did not bring them up, I doubt he
ever would. His father, a hardworking Irish immigrant who built up a
business single-handedly, moved his family from the inner city to the
world of suburban country clubs. However, as he was always at work,
he had little time to spend with his children. Steve's father pushed his
son to excel in academics so that he would be a success as well.

In an attempt to win his father's love and attention, Steve always
succeeded at school even when it meant working harder than anybody else. He also joined the tennis team, and through his hard work
went from barely making the squad to becoming the top-seeded
player. His father, however, was rarely able to make it to his tennis
matches because he worked such long hours, just as Steve does now.
Without his father's approval, Steve believes he is less intelligent than
others and becomes anxious when he has a chance to show off his
knowledge to colleagues or clients.

Yet Steve is a man who is passionate about many things, although
not people. He is an avid sports fan and music aficionado, and he en-
joys photography and painting. He also likes his work—and uses it to
avoid social engagements. Working the incredibly long hours that
make a social life very difficult, he sometimes leaves me messages
from his office at 2 a.m. to cancel our early-morning session the next
day. At other times he has come to our sessions after working until
midnight. Undoubtedly he genuinely feels some wish, albeit well buried, to be with me. But just as he may have experienced his father as
not really interested in him as a person, so too he might at times experience me as uninterested, as when I fell asleep.

If Steve's father is somewhat of an enigma, I am even less certain
about how Steve's mother fits into the picture. Despite my having

asked about her, she remains shrouded in mystery. Steve has called her a "loving" woman who also wanted him to succeed but who never put pressure on him. She never worked outside the home and presumably had plenty of time for both her children. Yet her absence from the treatment must have meaning. (Or perhaps her presence is taken for granted.) My countertransference—first my being interested in Steve and then becoming suddenly sleepy and distant—led me to a tentative formulation: any limited attention Steve had as an infant was redirected to his sister, who was born a year and a half later. His fear of being noticed may come from his childhood longing to be recognized for his own unique desires, a longing that was constantly being thwarted. The wish to connect with another may be equated with his desire for mother or father, a need that seems too frightening for him to acknowledge.

In fact, Steve's longings are so dissociated, he began therapy only when they forced themselves into his consciousness and overwhelmed him by surprise. He entered treatment because a male coworker on whom he had a crush had just been transferred to one of the company's offices in another part of the country. Steve was shocked at how this move devastated him. He was having difficulty sleeping and found himself crying when home alone. He had previously had a crush on a straight male colleague and a similarly strong reaction when that man left the firm.

With these two exceptions, Steve had been surprisingly successful at keeping his sexuality at bay. When he saw a handsome man on the street or on television, he would simply stop himself from feeling excited. When he did have sexual fantasies, he was always the receptive partner and had sex forced on him. For example, in one fantasy, he was held down and raped. In others, he was tied to a bed or chair. Occasionally, he would masturbate to these fantasies, but only infrequently.

Steve admitted his fantasies to me with great hesitation, and only after we both decided it might be helpful for him to be on the couch, because he could not look at me and talk about such things.

Steve and I have enacted his fantasy of being overpowered by me with some frequency: when I questioned him about being late; when I insisted he talk about our relationship; when I made him uncomfortable by bringing up his sex life or his being gay. In each of those instances, I felt like the aggressor, pinning him down and forcing him to submit to my will. I was left with a range of feelings—guilt, excitement, and self-blame for not taking a more careful role in his treatment. I sensed that Steve might be feeling similarly—guilty, excited, and angry with me for forcing myself on him. How much did he want me to keep my distance, and how much did he want me to push him to become the abusive, exciting rapist?

Steve's ambivalence, both toward me and the treatment, seemed evident in the fact that it was nearly two years before he reported his first dream: "I'm in Brooklyn with a client. We need to get to a function in Westchester [a suburban county of New York]. We are looking at a map. The client used to live in Westchester but now lives in Brooklyn, so he knows the way."

Steve's only association was that he felt fortunate to be in the presence of a client who could help him find his way. Clearly, there is an idealizing component to the transference. He had no particular thoughts about Brooklyn or Westchester, although I thought about the fact that my Brooklyn accent slips out sometimes and that very likely the patient heard it in our two years together.

"Could I be the client in the dream?" I asked.

"How could that be? It was specifically my client."

I explained to Steve about how everyone in the dream could represent either one of us. For that matter, Steve could be the client—after all he was the client here—and he could be feeling as if he needed to lead me because I did not know the way. He might feel frustrated by having to be both therapist and patient, as when I fell sleep and he continued free-associating until he ended the session. This interpretation, however, did not make an impression on him.

I told Steve that the dream might be about how we both wanted to find our way to more emotional intimacy. I worried that he would

equate intimacy with sex and shut down. But, to my surprise, he re-
lated how he had hugged his niece at a family gathering over the
weekend and that he found himself feeling teary as he did so. I too felt
wet-eyed, moved by Steve's unlikely emotional display, and, although
it seemed impossible that he could not see this, I decided to point it
out and ask if he had noticed. Typically, Steve said he had and
changed the subject.

Our sessions often had this quality. I frequently felt as if I were on
a roller-coaster ride; sometimes I felt connected to Steve, and other
times pushed away, bored, or even confused. I was having a hard time
keeping passion alive within me, much less finding it in Steve.

It was a reflection of the difficult time I was having in my work with
Steve that I presented his case for supervision in two different groups.
One group, led by an interpersonal psychoanalyst, suggested that I find
a way to help Steve talk about his disavowed aggression and desire—
which were felt within me—as a way to try to understand what was going on between us. The group also suggested I inquire about what his
fantasies were of my sexual orientation and my relationship to it and
also what he thought I wanted from him and for him.

The second group, led by an object relations analyst, offered a
completely different approach. They suggested I contain Steve's fra-
gility and his terror of being in the outside world. I should be curious
about all that is scary out there, but I should be careful not to force
myself on him. And, they suggested, I definitely should not push him
to talk about me and the transference—that desire was mine and is
too frightening for him right now.

Great. Two different groups were offering seemingly irreconcil-
able options. My inability to find a universal source of authority made
me think of Steve's own struggle to decide how he should live his
sexual identity.

As I grappled with the question of whether to confront or contain, Steve entered my office one winter morning and handed me a
check. As our fingers accidentally touched, a spark of static electricity
flew between them. This was too much to pass up.

"That was some spark between us," I said. "What was that like for you?"

Steve turned beet red. "It was uncomfortable," he said and then fell silent.

"What was uncomfortable about it?"

"Well, when you say there was a spark between us, it makes me feel like you're coming on to me," he said.

Steve had made this accusation before. But behind his fear was there also a wish? After all, hadn't Steve taken on the role of the rapist, tying me down by constantly changing the subject, coming late, and evading me with his frequent discomfort? I was having difficulty finding a way we could both bring up our loving and sexual feelings toward one another without each of us feeling raped.

To help us feel more connected, I began to talk with Steve about the possibility of his sitting up. At the beginning of treatment, lying down helped him tell me his shameful sexual fantasies. Now it seemed to be making Steve feel more isolated and avoidant. Sitting up and seeing me allowed Steve to feel a little more relaxed and open. It may also have helped him feel more able to defend himself and to assess my intentions better. Around this time, he had another dream:

> I was in the cast of *Dawson's Creek* and we were in a room with other people. A party, with a lot of drinking, was going on. The young male lead got sick and ran to the bathroom and I went after him. He was vomiting and I held him in a way that I was sexually attracted to him. Then the whole party broke up and someone said to me, "You didn't follow the script at that point." The actor recoiled from me and was uncomfortable with the way I was holding him.

Never before had Steve conveyed a sexual dream; it had been some time since he had had a sexual thought to report. Yet this event was again tempered by a pulling back, as Steve had few associations and wanted to move away as quickly as possible. I told him I thought it was important that this was the first sexual dream he had remembered and that his unconscious must be ready to deal with something that had been too frightening. I asked him if he had any thoughts or feelings about the sexual elements of the dream, but he had little to say about them.

I was also interested in the young age of the actor he found sexually attractive (I am several years younger than Steve) and wondered what it meant that he was vomiting. Was Steve sickened by his sexual thoughts, or did he worry they would make others sick? Was he commenting on the way my interpretations were spewing out?

Clearly, there was a sense that sexual feelings could lead to rejection and that they are not in our script. I thought about how Steve had told me he took comfort in our having "roles" (me as doctor, he as patient) whenever he thought I was coming on to him. The dream also spoke to his great fear that I would recoil from him if he showed any interest—a good reason for him to protest my coming on to him when we both felt excited. Was he afraid I would be disgusted by his sexual feelings, in general and for me?

Yet despite these concerns, I sensed that Steve was beginning to recognize me as a separate subject of desire. After all, he was attracted to the other actor in the dream. And when, a few weeks later, I announced the dates of my summer vacation, Steve asked if I would be going someplace that was fun. It was the first time he had ever asked about my vacation plans. I told him I would be going to China, a place that aroused the interests of most of my other patients. He said simply okay and moved on. Once again, he had shown his longing, for once, his curiosity about me, and then had become frightened or jealous and changed the subject. His moving away from his interest in me was all the more jarring since this was a possible point of contact between us; Steve is an avid traveler who has been to many exotic places (usually alone). I told him that I sensed he was ambivalent about knowing anything about me, and yet it was he who had brought up where I was going. So part of him was curious just as a part of him was frightened. I wanted to learn more about both parts, I said. I suggested that, when he gets in touch with his desire, it frightens him; so he has to cut it off and experience it as coming from me. For once, Steve did not protest. Instead, he said only that he found my idea "interesting."

Steve's wish to see more of me, despite great ambivalence, was evident in another dream he had at this time:

> Someone tells me that you've been an expert witness in some litigation and the case is successful because of you. I'm surprised. I didn't know you did this as part of your work. Then this person says you had throat cancer surgery and have survived that. In session, I both want to see where the surgery was—I can see there's a mark that's been there all along—but I don't want to see and embarrass you.

Steve's not wanting to see and embarrass me made me think of how he had reacted when I slept. Yet there was a part of him that wants to see me, even with my scars and vulnerabilities. While he might be wondering whether I am a competent person, or a sick person, or both, he was beginning to see me as an expert witness—an important role for a man whose needs went unnoticed as a child. Or perhaps being noticed may have felt too over stimulating.

My growing ability to sense Steve's vulnerability was evident during a recent session, when, in a moment of reverie, I suddenly thought of vanilla pudding and how I have always been fascinated by the thin skin on top. It is so easy to break through the skin, that flimsy but necessary barrier to getting to the desired sweetness within. I began to think about this as a metaphor for Steve's interpersonal style. He had erected a thin layer of protection around himself in an attempt to keep the world out and to maintain his own fragile sense of internal integrity. I thought about how thin and flimsy this protection must have felt, which must be why he withdrew so quickly and deeply within himself whenever he showed any desire. I thought of the way he must have experienced me as constantly poking at that thin layer and how vulnerable he must have felt around me. I did not make any interpretations, but reflected on just how frightened he must feel in the world. To be cognizant of and hold his vulnerability, I needed to have more moments like this when I could identify it within myself.

In the next session, Steve arrived 10 minutes late and said he needed to leave 15 minutes early to get to work for a meeting. I wondered if my getting in touch with his vulnerability in the previous session had unconsciously frightened him. Or had it opened up something within him that was difficult to deal with or share? In the few minutes that remained, he told me how he had been "swept away" seeing the musical *Oklahoma!* He was moved to tears when, during the overture, the waltz "Out of My Dreams" suddenly and unexpectedly glided out of a cowboy tune. "Out of My Dreams": the title again made me think of my falling asleep. "It felt familiar," Steve said. "I no longer felt lonely. I was moved not by the words, but by the melody."

The challenge I face with Steve is to be swept away in his sadness, isolation, and homophobia and to hold all of that without having to put it into jarring words. But doing this is quite difficult for me, not just because Steve is so good at shutting me out. One of Steve's fears, which he repeats with great regularity, is that my agenda is to make him gay. He has a point. I come on so strong, I think, because I do wish to help him become more comfortable with, and, yes, act on his sexuality. This may not be the patient's agenda, but when I look deeply within myself, I have to admit it is sometimes mine.

One reason for wanting Steve to embrace his sexuality may be a conscious identification from my own coming-out experience. Steve countertransferentially represents me in my adolescence, when I knew I was gay but was too intimidated to tell anyone, much less act on my sexuality. It was difficult for me to endure his pain, which was so like the pain I felt as a teenager in the closet. I am filled with the wish that Steve recognize both me and his homosexuality. Yet I often manage to convince myself that I have no agenda for him at all.

My strong identification with Steve's dissociated homosexuality helps explain why I fell asleep earlier in the treatment. Then, too,

Steve was doing a good job of keeping me at a distance. Yet despite that enactment—and possibly because of it—Steve and I have continued with the work and have begun to touch on areas of vulnerability. My sleepiness helped wake me up to just how detached from and frightened Steve is of connection. And it may have provided Steve with both a familiar and a new experience. I fell asleep on Steve much as his parents had when he was growing up. This reenactment must have been painful for him. And yet, unlike his parents, I could also wake up and show great interest in Steve and what had happened between us. I communicated a desire to know Steve and to understand our interaction. This possibility may have been frightening for him, but it may also have given him the message that he is worth caring about and that another person can show interest in him without overstimulating him.

Considering his age and his fear, Steve may never act on his sexuality. I have to accept this is a real possibility without considering myself a failed therapist. But I cannot possibly know what will happen until we get there together. I can only be more comfortable with Steve's vulnerability and conflict about his sexuality, rather than push him in any one direction.

Steve has made life decisions, including how he lives as a gay man, that are different than mine. Can I open myself up to accept this, without forever playing out his fantasy and forcing my will on him? Is there a way I can work with Steve's formidable internalized homophobia without having my own get in the way? There have been some recent positive signs of his slowly opening up to me—bringing in the dream with sexual desire, and his story about *Oklahoma!* As we continue our work, the question remains: Can we find a way to be swept away together or will unrequited desire be our only refrain?

8

HOMOEROTIC COUNTERTRANSFERENCE
The Love That Dares Not Speak Its Name?

Recently a patient I had been working with for about two years, a gay man named Kevin, brought in a mini–photo album he had compiled of his recently deceased grandmother. In our previous session, Kevin had talked about wanting to show me the album so I could see the beloved grandmother who had helped raise him. Obviously, there was much he wished to show me about himself—and to learn about me from my reaction. However, I was little prepared for the exact Polaroid moment that would soon ensue.

Kevin's mood was bouncy as he walked into my office that day. He sat up on the couch instead of lying down as he normally did. "I brought it," he said, smiling as he held the small book in front of him. At the time, I sat in a desk chair on wheels a few feet to the side and slightly behind the couch. By the way Kevin had set up the situation, I had at least three immediate options: I could make the safe decision to analyze what his feelings were about bringing in the album; I could take the album from him and look through it from the distance of where I normally sit; or I could roll closer to him so that we could look at the album together, side by side, which is what he appeared to want. I hesitated for a moment, wanting to accept his invitation, but also uncomfortable. What boundaries was I about to cross? I looked at the expression of eager anticipation on Kevin's face and realized that I, too, longed for more closeness with this challenging patient who rightly complained about my distance yet maintained his own. Nervously, I rolled my chair over.

Kevin handed me the album, and, as I turned the pages, he narrated the photos with interesting background stories. Initially, I felt awkward sitting so close to him, but I quickly relaxed as I became more and more intrigued by the photos of Kevin and his vibrant-looking grandmother. I became so engrossed in the album and in Kevin's enlightening narration that I almost forgot I was an analyst in the midst of a pivotal moment with a patient.

And then it happened. I turned the page and there was a photo, taken a number of years earlier, of Kevin and his grandmother on the beach. The woman had on a blouse and shorts, but Kevin was wearing only a bathing suit. There was nothing lewd, provocative, or particularly sexual about the photo. In fact, lacking much muscular definition and wearing baggy trunks, Kevin looked far more boyish than buff. Yet, with his tan and a relaxed smile that showed just a touch of cockiness, I found him unexpectedly sensual. There was something soft and vulnerable, yet seductively erotic, about the half-naked Kevin. Now, I have felt sexual excitement before with patients, but never as I sat so close to them and rarely so unexpectedly and forcefully. My mind began to race as fast as my heart. Could Kevin see how I was staring at the photo? Did he sense my excitement and discomfort? Could he tell I had a slight erection? What did my titillation and embarrassment—my sense that sexual feelings had almost been thrust upon me—tell me about Kevin and the transference? Most important, what should I do or say?

I shall return to this tense and important moment later in the chapter. But first some history.

Kevin had entered therapy almost two years prior to his grandmother's death. At the time, his life was in turmoil. His mother was beginning to deteriorate from Alzheimer's disease and his grandmother was growing increasingly frail. Each woman required increased attention and support from Kevin. His father, who had left when Kevin was a boy, was long out of the picture, and a younger brother refused to help. In addition, Kevin had entered treatment because he was about to move in with his boyfriend, Edward, and he was excited—and petrified. He had a history of brief relationships in which he experienced feeling bored as soon as things became intimate. At that point, his sexual interest in his partner would wane, and Kevin, usually hooking up with other men on the Internet, would begin frequent, anonymous one-night stands. He would then break off the longer standing relationship. Already he was noticing this pattern with Edward. To make matters worse, shortly after Kevin began treatment, Edward was diagnosed HIV-positive. Kevin, who had been positive himself (but healthy) for many years, now had another sick person for whom he had to care. The desire to flee was great.

Sensing the need to deal with this issue, he had purposely sought out a gay male therapist with whom he assumed he would feel more comfortable and accepted. Yet, for most of the first two years of treatment, we rarely discussed his sex life. There were so many crises to deal with, particularly as his mother's and grandmother's health further deteriorated. Looking back, I believe I was more than eager to take on the role of caretaker and put off issues about his sex life, especially fantasies that he hinted at were violent and disturbing to him. In a way, we were both colluding to keep his sexual feelings out of the room. It was if we were allowing his ill mother and grandmother— even his lover—to act as chaperones, their presence in the treatment ensuring that nothing sexual would come up between us.

Then, with the death of his grandmother, came the photograph in the bathing suit.

As I sat with Kevin I stalled until I could regain my equanimity. Without commenting on the bathing suit photo, I turned the page. If Kevin had a reaction, I did not notice. Regaining my composure, I began to think again with some degree of levelheadedness, even analytic curiosity. I thought about what it meant that Kevin was allowing me to see more of him, showing me his body, himself as a sexual being. I wondered why I was so disturbed about seeing him this way. It began to dawn on me that I must have been resisting noticing Kevin's sexuality for some time. Why had I only vaguely been aware of Kevin's boyish good looks before?

Suddenly, I began to remember times I *had* thought about him as a sexual being. There were even a few sessions, I now remembered, when he brushed close to me on the way out. I had felt a momentary flutter inside me but then quickly forgot about it. That is not like me. What was this behavior saying about the patient's sexual dissociation (and my own, for that matter)? Had I been avoiding recognizing this response because there was something disturbing about Kevin's sexuality that I did not want to see? I later thought about how much Kevin had complained of what he considered my strict adherence to boundaries—particularly the time I ended a session on time, despite his being in the middle of a crying episode. Had Kevin been trying to seduce me into loosening the boundaries all along, and was I afraid of what would happen if I was not careful? How complicated it all seemed!

When I had finished going through the album, I rolled my chair back. I asked what it was he wished me to see.

"Oh, I just wanted you to see what my grandmother looked like."

"I also think you wanted me to see more of who you are," I said. "I have a feeling there are sides of you we've both been avoiding—your sexuality and the fantasies you've mentioned that frighten you. I think you may have been experiencing me as being too uneasy to look also. But I think we can find a way for both of us to work on this."

It was with much apprehension and uncertainty that I made this comment. Although it seemed important to deal with the split-off sexual feelings I sensed I might be experiencing through projective identification, I was unsure how to bring them into the room. I knew that bringing up his sexuality, and particularly my own avoidance, might be experienced as jarring, threatening, or seductive. What would I say if Kevin asked if I was having sexual feelings? I also worried that my sudden assertiveness might be a sexualized enactment of something of which I was not yet aware. Maybe I was acting on my anxiety about sexual feelings by refusing to sit with them, instead forcing them on Kevin before he was ready. But I thought that not saying something would further communicate to the patient that his feelings were too frightening and overwhelming for both of us. I realized how complicated this moment was, and I braced for what I anticipated would be Kevin's agitated response.

In fact, Kevin surprised me. "Hmm," he sighed. "I don't know." Then he grew silent. After a moment, he mumbled in a groggy voice, "I don't understand this. I'm feeling very sleepy all of a sudden."

It occurred to me that my comment and the feelings I possibly evoked might have temporarily overwhelmed Kevin, who was reacting by dissociating. Yet while he drifted in and out of a foggy state for much of the remaining session, he was also able to express some surprise and curiosity about his "strange" reaction, although whenever I attempted to understand it with him, he would immediately become sleepy again. The sleepiness seemed like a warning sign not to push too hard. However, I also felt it was important to continue carefully trying to engage his curiosity, to avoid further avoidance. There was something freeing for me—and I intuitively felt even for my groggy patient—in being able to confront what had so long been taboo. Relying on my own feelings, I drew attention to the fact that part of Kevin wanted to introduce sexual material into the treatment, but part of him, the part that was sleepy now, was frightened. I said firmly that it was time we started looking at things we had been avoiding, frightening as they might be. I suggested he try not to fall asleep and I would try not to let him.

I anticipated the next session with a mixture of eagerness and un-certainty. I did not know what state Kevin would be in—foggy, angry, agitated? I suspected he might act as if nothing had happened. Once again, Kevin surprised me. He seemed relaxed and curious. The first thing he said was, "Boy, that was really weird the way I kept falling asleep last time, huh?"

So began a delicate process of looking at Kevin's shame around his sexuality and his fear that I would find his fantasies and activities disgusting. Slowly, as his shame and resistances loosened, he began to share details of his sex life, including how he liked to verbally humili-ate his willing partner. This made him feel excited and in control. I sensed he was increasingly feeling the same with me, since, where once he had been cautious and distant, he now exhibited a flirtatious bravado. He would gently (and sometimes not so gently) kid me, teas-ing me about how smiling more would not kill me. At times I felt toyed with and on guard, but mostly I, too, felt excited hearing about his sex life. I was surprised that I liked this cocky, humiliating side of my patient. I very much looked forward to our sessions. I felt like a willing sex partner engaged in a secret, special, and slightly "dirty" encounter.

Then, one day, Kevin's tone suddenly turned matter-of-fact. His embarrassment returned as he told me that he enjoyed urinating and defecating on an anonymous sexual partner. He especially liked "eat-ing out his partner's ass." I was disturbed by an image of Kevin defe-cating on (and eating the excrement of) someone. I think I resisted imagining that, symbolically, that someone could be me.

Perhaps Kevin perceived not only my discomfort, but also that I was interested in hearing more. As the session came to an end, he talked about how he wanted to share some of his fantasies, but that he was too embarrassed. The next week, on the way to his session, Kevin and I happened to ride up together in my office building's notoriously slow elevator. Normally, I dread being trapped with a patient for 16 floors, but today I felt relaxed and playful. When Kevin did not recognize me as he rushed through the closing elevator doors, it was I who now felt in control. "Weren't planning on saying hello?" I teased. When we got to the office, he told me how much he liked my letting down my guard in the elevator. Seeing this side of me helped him feel that he could finally tell me about his fantasies.

Kevin shared that he fantasized tying up another man—preferably a straight man—calling him a faggot and watching him squirm. But nothing got him more excited than the thought of tying up an adolescent boy and raping him. The idea also frightened him, not because he thought he would ever act on it, but surely because there must have been something wrong with him to have such fantasies. At that moment, he turned around on the couch and looked at me. "I think I'm making you uncomfortable," he said, adding that he sensed I was repulsed by his dirty thoughts and actions.

Although there was a great deal of projection in this statement, Kevin was also correct about my discomfort. The wave of nausea I had felt when he talked about defecating on other men had returned. Now I was even more disturbed by his fantasies of raping boys. My discomfort was the opposite of my original feeling of arousal at seeing the adolescent-looking Kevin in the photo. I realized that we were in the midst of an enactment that had actually been initiated many months before. Nonetheless, I still worried that I had made a mistake by opening up this area of exploration. Maybe I would only encourage him to rape a minor. For the first time, I began to feel that Kevin was tying my hands and defecating on me.

At first, I felt panicky and angry at myself for having opened up a Pandora's box that now seemed dangerous and out of control. However, then I began to think that Kevin might be conveying just what it was like to feel angry, helpless, guilt-ridden, and out of control. He was inviting me into his fantasies. He wanted to know whether I could withstand his "dirtiness," whether I would allow myself to be a willing partner in this messy, uncertain exploration (even to be defecated on symbolically) and not be repulsed. Or maybe I did need to feel repulsed, since he might be trying to evacuate the reaction to his dirty, sadistic fantasies into me.

I also began to wonder if part of my disgust was a defense against my own potential feelings of sexual excitement at being tied up and controlled. I was buoyed by Kevin's growing sense of trust, his being able to expose these shameful dissociated feelings to me. Ever since we had begun talking about his sex life and fantasies, there had been a growing integration of his sex life outside—he was having fewer anonymous encounters, and he had started talking about sex more with Edward and in couples therapy.

I told Kevin that some of what he had told me did, in fact, make me uncomfortable. I could understand why having these fantasies frightened him. But I also was confident we could both not only tolerate them, but explore what made them enjoyable as well. The fantasies were telling us about important aspects of his life. Kevin had reported nothing about sexual abuse when he was a boy, yet he had also said he had few memories from his childhood. Working on the theory that these fantasies were the products of actual experience, I wondered about what was being enacted in these experiences of control and humiliation—what might have happened to him as a boy that he was playing out?

When I asked, he mentioned in a matter-of-fact tone the time he worked with his stepfather, Fred, at a restaurant when Kevin was 14. One day, when everyone else had left, Fred told Kevin he could drive the car home if he gave him a blow job. Kevin, who yearned to feel the freedom of both driving and acting on his shameful same-sex fantasies—as well as having the acceptance of his distant stepfather—agreed. Yet the memory all seemed very hazy, and Kevin could recall no feelings. He had no other memories of sex with Fred, yet he and this stepfather were alone at the restaurant many times, and he had a sense that they had had sex on more than one occasion.

About this time, I was preparing to open a second office in New Jersey. Although I had been seeing Kevin in Manhattan, I offered to see him at the new office since he lived nearby. I explained that my office was in my home and wondered what that would be like for him. The idea pleased him, not only for the convenience, but also because he realized he would be getting more of a peek inside my life. I thought about the bathing suit photo. Only now he would be seeing more of me, and this made me feel nervous and vulnerable.

I was taken aback, then, when during the first session Kevin mentioned nothing about the new setting and instead told me how depressed he was. At first I withdrew, feeling hurt that I had exposed myself by inviting him into my home and had been rejected. (Had Kevin felt the same when I had had such a strong reaction to him in his bathing suit but instead had initially acted as if I hadn't noticed?) Then I began to wonder if being inside the place where I lived and had sex could be so stimulating that Kevin needed to dissociate. I mentioned my surprise that he had seemed oblivious to being in my home and wondered if his lack of interest in this new, more intimate setting had to do with his feeling depressed. He admitted he had had many fantasies about seeing my home and finding out more about me. He had arrived 20 minutes early, in fact, but from his car had looked at the outside of my house in the hope of seeing inside. He noticed that the blinds on all the windows were closed, even on the upstairs windows. He felt terribly let down. "You had hoped to peek inside and see more about me," I said, "but I had closed all the blinds. Even the blinds on the second floor, where you would assume my bedroom is." Kevin blushed and smiled, "As soon as you mentioned your bedroom, I had an image of you having sex."

I asked him to say more about this image. He became nervous and defensive. He did not see anything specific, he said. Just the idea of my having sex. Gently, I asked him whom I was with. I felt a little guilty about entangling my partner in this sordid affair and a little nervous about opening myself up to the sexual fantasies of a man who fantasized about raping boys. Kevin responded in a more playful tone, "You're with your lover, of course. Unless you're being bad on the side."

"Am I being bad like you?" I asked. I also thought, "Bad with you?" "Oh, no, I can't imagine you doing anything bad—you're too much of a choir boy," he said. "Now Dr. A," he added, referring to the psychiatrist to whom I had referred him for medication, "I can see him being a pig. There's something very dirty and sexual about him."

"You can see Dr. A being a pig, but not me," I said. "Maybe there's something safe about seeing me as a choir boy. It means you don't have to think about me in a sexual way. And yet your sexual fantasies *are* about choir boys."

Kevin smiled delightedly at my comment and said, "Well, well, well . . . maybe you are a pig!" Maybe I had different sides to me— sweet and innocent, but also raunchy, like him.

When the patient arrived an uncharacteristic five minutes late for his next session, I worried that I had pushed too hard in the previous hour. I felt guilty and wondered if I was enacting the role of the step-father, seducing my ambivalent patient. Apologizing for being late, Kevin said, "I had the day off. I was sitting around watching TV in my underwear and I completely lost track of the time!" An image of Kevin in his skivvies came into my mind, a picture that was by no means unpleasant. What was he telling me about where we were going to go together with such a provocative statement? Kevin said he was eager to talk further about the incident with his stepfather. He had more memories of the incident at the restaurant—it was not just that Kevin had given Fred a blow job, they had also engaged in "69." He also remembered a time when he had attempted anal intercourse with Fred, but Kevin was too frightened and could not maintain an erection (just as he had trouble as an adult during sex with his part-ner). As he lay on the couch now, visualizing the scene in the restau-rant, he visibly shuddered and said he could actually smell Fred—the nauseating odor of his anus and his uncircumcised penis. He remem-bered that, as the two of them drove home to dinner, Fred said, "Wash your hands when you get in, so your mother won't smell anything."

Kevin and I have only just begun to explore his guilt at hurting his mother by secretly having sex with her husband. He has talked about how angry he is at Fred. We have also started to deal with Kevin's ter-rific need for acceptance and validation from Fred, his father, and others as he was growing up—feelings that still make him feel weak and needy today. During a recent session, he spoke quite movingly about how, for the first time in his life, he feels he has allowed himself to feel vulnerable and to be supported by me. As he spoke, I suddenly found myself moved to tears at the thought of being a good, loving father to my scared but appreciative young son. There was nothing sexual about this fantasy; I was feeling only protective. The image shifted quickly to a more erotic one as Kevin said proudly that he felt stronger than ever and no longer had the need to connect sexually with strangers so much, or even to masturbate. When he said this, I had a brief image of him masturbating and so quickly felt ashamed of myself that I blinked it out of my mind. How had my counter-transference shifted so fast from paternal to erotic? Had the patient sensed a seductive side to my paternal fantasy of which I was un-aware? And why was I suddenly so ashamed of having sexual feelings when this sensation had previously been so pleasurable?

As I thought about these questions, I was particularly interested in understanding the nature of Kevin's sadomasochistic fantasies; and how we enacted them in moments of emotional closeness, followed by excitement, then shame and disgust. I believe they are typical of the kinds of enactments, dissociation, and splitting around sexuality that are common in the work with gay clients in particular, but proba-bly with most patients in general.

I understand Kevin's need to dominate and control as defensively having originated in very early experiences of shame and humiliation. I believe these painful feelings, as well as his conflicted desires for closeness and acceptance, have long been dissociated. They were now being enacted with me, his partner, and the men he meets anony-mously. Initially, Kevin had described his youth in a vague but ideal-ized fashion. His allegedly wholesome, happy childhood was a far cry from what was being represented in both the transference–counter-transference and the patient's sadomasochistic sex life and fantasies.

As I probed, a fuller picture began to emerge. First came the terror and humiliation Kevin had felt in school, particularly in the shower after gym class. There the other boys gathered around and teased him mercilessly as a "faggot" for his lack of athletic skills, his boyish body, and what he, too, considered his lack of masculinity. A similar scene was then repeated at home. The patient's father called him "faggot" and "sissy," humiliated him in front of his family over the dinner table, and exposed his horrible secret of being gay. To compensate and feel in control, Kevin fantasized about getting even. He would beat up his tormentors and humiliate them by calling them the same names they called him. In his fantasies, he felt strong and masculine. He dissociated from the idea of himself as the weak and feeble boy in the gym and identified as the other—the tied-up adult, the raped child, the helpless one who felt the pain. Also split off was his desire to be connected with the other boys, to be loved and accepted by his father, to feel masculine and comfortable with his gay sexual feelings. As is typical of many gay adolescents, Kevin learned to compartmentalize his shameful feelings about sex and intimacy, and eroticized his friendships with other boys. In fact, he had been having a long-term sexual relationship with his closest friend from age 12. Paradoxically this relationship filled him not only with further feelings of shame, but also with a sense of being lovable, valued, and strong.

Initially, Kevin had no understanding about why he had such florid fantasies of humiliating others; he had been surprised at becoming aware of just how humiliated he had felt as a boy. Defecating and urinating on others—and also eating (taking in) the excrement of others—were ways he expressed his desire to evacuate his worthless sense of self, as well as submissive expressions of desires to surrender (Ghent, 1990), to be able to integrate them, to be known by the other, and to find his true self.

Clearly, the issues around excitement, shame, and dissociation were continually enacted with me. At times, I became the humiliating father/classmates (e.g., my reaction of disgust to his rape fantasy and his enjoyment of excrement), the abused boy (my hurt feelings when

Kevin did not acknowledge my home), the seductive stepfather (too quickly offering to lower my fee when he lost his job), the choir boy avoiding sexual feelings, and the "dirty" sex partner enjoying our badness but then feeling guilty and ashamed. Kevin has also taken on all these roles in the transference. For instance, I am aware of the parallels between his nausea at the smell of Fred's anus and penis and my own queasiness as he told me of defecating on someone and eating out of their anus. Each of us gets in touch with feeling sexual, cocky, excited, and in control, but these feelings can quickly turn to shame and "dirtiness."

I have often thought about why I am alternately excited and then repulsed by the "dirtiness" of Kevin's sexuality. Although these may be aspects of projective identification, I believe the enactments are so strong because Kevin is expressing sexually aggressive sides of myself that I also find exciting, yet embarrassing, and from which I tend to dissociate. I believe I am jealous of his ability to act on them; his assessment of me as a choir boy is not inaccurate. When he expresses these aggressive, dirty feelings, they are at first safe for me, since I get to remain in the choir yet still live vicariously through the devil. Both Kevin and I can become aroused in treatment, but then dissociate from our shameful homoerotic desires and see this excitement as something that has sullied a more "clean" sense of love, intimacy, and desire.

Intersubjectively, I believe Kevin notices when he has this effect on me; often it causes him to withdraw temporarily, afraid of my judgment and confirmation of his "dirtiness." Other times, he becomes angry, playing out his sadistic revenge fantasy of tying me up symbolically and defecating on me through angry or caustic statements. He also is able to experience me as clearly interested, present, and willing to take on the aggressive role myself from time to time, and gently but firmly pushing him to continue when he is frightened. I believe my continued interest in Kevin's erotic life has given him a new realization that sex does not have to be shameful. Furthermore, he can bring together desire and intimacy in a way he is only just beginning to achieve with his partner.

And it all began with a not so innocent photo of a young man and his grandmother on the beach, and an analyst suddenly caught in the middle of an erotically charged enactment.

9

WHEN PUSH COMES TO SHOVE
Domination, Submission, and the
Hands-Tied Analyst

With his sweet, freckled face and shy smile, Adam looked like the boy next door. Although he was 32 years old, you might have guessed he was five years younger. His preppy clothes and his natural good looks made him seem as if he had just stepped out of a male fashion catalog.

But if Adam were the boy next door, then the neighborhood must have been zoned for an S&M parlor. From the very first session, he described a history of drinking and then going online or to a leather bar, where he enjoyed hooking up with another man and being urinated on or slapped and spit on while having sex. One of his major fantasies was playing a naughty son being spanked by his angry father. It would be a while before I could understand the meanings of these sexual activities. At first, Adam recited them as if he

meant simply to titillate me and grab my attention. If so, he succeeded on both counts.

After a recent drinking and sex binge, Adam entered Alcoholics
Anonymous and got my phone number through an organization in
the gay community. He had been in therapy once previously but,
amazingly, had kept his drinking and sex life secret from his therapist,
a woman whom he described as "Freudian" and who apparently said
little in session. He had wanted to please her and make her like him
and in doing so may have enacted another masochistic situation in
which he was spending thousands of dollars—and a year of his time—
without any hope of getting better.

Nonetheless, if he had spent a year not talking about his drinking
and sexual fantasies with his former therapist, I had to wonder why he
was he being so open *now,* with me. Had he reached the point of desperation, where he was willing to be honest? Was there something in-
herent in me that he saw he could trust? Did he assume from the
referral source that I was gay and thus had an advantage over a presumably straight, female therapist?

As I listened to Adam's history, I soon learned more about where
his fantasies came from, particularly his fantasy of being spanked and
admonished by an angry father. Adam had grown up the seventh of
eight children in an Italian Catholic family. He described a bleak
childhood during which his parents—both alcoholics—had little
time for him. He said that both parents were harsh, although his
mother was sullen and brooding, whereas his father often beat the
children. Adam experienced some of these beatings as sexual. He remembered his father's forcing him to pull his own pants down in
front of the entire family and hitting him across the bottom with a
belt—a scene repeatedly reenacted in Adam's S&M fantasies. He particularly remembered the time his father came out of the bathroom
naked and began punching Adam's older brother. His father's naked-
ness embarrassed him; I wondered if it might also have been exciting.
Adam became visibly uncomfortable as he described showering with

his father and brother on at least one occasion when he was five years old. He said he felt excited yet also uncomfortable around his father's uncircumcised penis, which was so different looking and so much more imposing than his own.

For the most part, however, Adam escaped the worst of the beatings by taking on the role of a good boy who blended into the background and did as his parents instructed. He learned to need little and to ask for less. He worked hard on his chores and, as an adolescent, helped his father in his lumber business. Rarely did his father show appreciation—the hard work was expected—but at least Adam escaped the kind of beatings inflicted on his brothers.

My formulation was that Adam had grown up in a harsh, violent atmosphere in which being the good boy was a necessity if he was to avoid beatings that took on a sexualized nature with his father. Being good, however, also made him feel left out and ignored as well as jealous of his brothers, who, while being beaten, got more attention than he did. Consequently, he repeated scenes of humiliation and submission in the sexual beatings he received now as an adult. I saw these fantasy beatings as an attempt to connect with a father who was present only in a brutal, distant way.

Adam and I had our own submission and domination enactment from the very beginning. It initially took place in the setting of the fee. At my suggestion (to please me?), Adam wished to come more than once a week. His insurance, however, would pay only a tiny amount per session, and he did not have enough money to pay my full fee once a week, let alone to pay to come twice a week or more. He wanted to get the lowest fee possible but then worried that I would be angry at him and would retaliate against him, just as his father would do. The negotiations were excruciating and lasted for several weeks. If he agreed to five dollars too much, I won; five dollars too little meant he won, which also meant he lost, since I would seek vengeance. Adam told me he thought that if I did something for him, I would be doing it because I was supposed to and I would end up resenting it. Or he would have to be a really good patient to earn it. One up, one down—someone was always on top and someone was always humiliated. I asked who was one up in our relationship.

"I think that's fairly obvious," he said.

"Humor me," I said.

"You are. You set the fee. You decide the cancellation policy. I spill my guts while you sit silently and tell me nothing about yourself. You're the one with all the power in this relationship."

"Is that at all exciting?" I asked. I knew the patient found it exciting to be slapped around during sex, and I wondered if he felt the same way with me. Also, although our negotiations around the fee, my cancellation policy, and other issues were not always easy, I did find them exciting. They had almost a sexual charge.

"It's mostly scary," said Adam, in response to whether he was excited by my power. "You can hurt me if I'm not careful and let you get too close."

"But don't you find it exciting being hurt in your sexual play?" At this point, I was so wrapped up in my own countertransference excitement that I was not listening to the patient, who was clearly telling me he was not titillated but, rather, was frightened by what I would do with my power. Unconsciously engaging in an enactment, I was countertransferentially exercising my power to push my ideas and my own feelings on the patient, who had little choice but to fight back or capitulate. Adam chose to hold his ground.

"But this isn't sexual, and I don't trust you well enough yet."

Adam's candor, and his ability to be playful and introspective and work within the transference, made him a gratifying, seductive patient. I wondered if his last therapist had experienced him the same way—if he was being a good boy for me, if he was showing the sides he thought I wanted to see but was not showing me the whole picture. It had been some time since he had spoken about sex; he claimed he was not having any.

As our work progressed, I was left with mixed feelings. Partly I felt placed on a pedestal—powerful and perfect, but mostly, well protected from Adam's anger. But it did not take long before I found myself aware of feeling sadistic toward him. Adam had a way of being very good and yet asking for a lot at the same time. He wanted my home phone number, for instance, as if I were an AA sponsor. When I did not give it to him, he arrived 10 minutes late for our next session. His habit of arriving up to 20 minutes late when he was angry with me about something that had come up in the previous session only fueled my sadistic feelings.

Then one day a fly buzzed into the office through an open window. We both stared at the annoying fly as it buzzed around the consultation room. Finally, it lit on the floor between us and perched for a few precious, quiet seconds. I looked at Adam and said, "Would you like to do the honors, or should I?"

"Go right ahead," said Adam, although I am not sure he knew quite what I had in mind. With one quick move, I squashed the bug with my foot. I have to admit, I even surprised myself. I am either more agile than I thought, or this was one slow bug. "Yes!" I yelled jubilantly.

For a moment, Adam look stunned. "I can't believe you did that. You certainly took a lot of pleasure from killing a fly. You really are a sadist."

"And you weren't thinking of doing the same thing?" I asked.

"No. Well, maybe. I don't know."

"Ah, maybe you have your own sadistic side. Of course, I do think you identify outwardly with the fly. After all, you've identified me as the powerful one. I think you sometimes feel as though you're under my size-11 shoes."

"You wear size-11 shoes? You must have really big feet."

"You know what they say about big feet," I said. The comment slipped out before I had a chance to think about its possibly overstimulating him.

Adam flashed a devilish smile that seemed incongruous on his angelic face. "Ooh, you're filthy! You're the kind of sadist I could get to like."

It was the first time Adam and I could be playful with each other without the danger of either of us being humiliated. But it was a moment we could not sustain. Although I felt enlivened, Adam quickly began to pull away. He blushed and suddenly turned serious. When I asked what had happened, he said that he felt embarrassed. He did not feel comfortable engaging in sexual banter with his therapist. He might be able to talk about sex *to* me, but my active participation was too much like having it.

Nonetheless, Adam became more open after the incident with the fly. He said he was surprised to see me take pleasure in my sadism since part of my power came from my being so composed while he felt so vulnerable. The incident had two immediate effects: it made him willing to talk in more detail about his sexual life, and it created more of a sense of closeness between us. My display of sexual playfulness and aggression showed that I would be willing to enter his world of domination and submission without flinching or judging him. My showing more sides to myself enabled him to risk showing more sides of himself. We discussed how talking about the kind of charged sex he had enjoyed while he was drinking might threaten his sobriety. However, at nine months into the therapy, those efforts seemed less of a danger.

And so Adam invited me into his sexual world. He told me why he enjoyed getting urinated on, slapped, and devalued. He found it exciting to give himself over totally to a powerful other whom he could trust not to hurt him. He felt powerful himself—he could cause pleasure by submitting, and he could cause pain and disappointment at any point if he stopped playing the game.

When he was having sex, Adam felt both needed and in control. Although he assumed the role of beggar, his partner was also left begging for more, even if this aspect was unspoken. Adam's ability to excite his partner so greatly made him feel special, a feeling he did not come by easily in his nonsexual life. Although his partner seemed to be in control, Adam felt the experience to be wonderfully mutual. There was a rhythm to the sex—each person could look into the other's eyes and know just how far to push the thin line between pleasure and pain. That the other was anonymous and that the play lacked conventional intimacy also allowed Adam to escape his fear of dependency.

Adam often spoke about being afraid of becoming dependent on me and then being let down when he needed me. That is what had happened with his parents. I also speculated that playing the bad boy to the angry father was his way of being found by his father—and finally getting the man's attention—so that he could master the trauma of childhood violence and neglect. No longer did he have to blend into the woodwork and watch with horror, jealousy, and sexual excitement as his brothers got all the attention. Love in Adam's family meant being slapped and yelled at. It is no surprise that he chose to recreate this situation in a safe way in his sex life.

Adam's sex play also had another function. Most of the time, he felt that no one could know all of him. Everyone just saw the hardworking, pleasant, eager-to-please boy next door. Domination and submission was a way to break out of that mold, to be known differently—as a bad boy, but also as a victim, a person in pain.

Interestingly, Adam's one relationship had been with an abusive man who devalued him in everyday life but not during sex. As a matter of fact, their sex life was quite boring, and toward the end of the year they spent together almost nonexistent. Adam learned to split the rest of his life from his sex life so that he could take pleasure only from anonymous sex and apparently recreate the role of the abused boy only in a way that left him feeling degraded in his nonsexual relationships.

As Adam described the sexual underground, I was surprised at how exciting I found it. Here was a world about which I knew little. There was something about being so "in sync" with one's partner, enjoying so much the delicious power of being submissive, that I could see its being a turn-on. Was this what Adam wanted, to turn me on and place me in the submissive position of begging to hear more?

The themes of dominance and submission, closeness and vulnerability, were the backdrop to most of treatment. They did not, however, always have the mutuality of his sex life. At the end of one session, Adam commented about seeing me as God and wanting to please me. I said, "You want to make me into God, but then I think you end up feeling inferior, unlike what happens in your sex life, where you feel you are more of an equal."

Adam was particularly sensitive to the ending of sessions, when he often felt cut off. When he began to feel this way, he would turn the tables. Rather than being the powerless, submissive one who was dependent on me, he would arrive late for the next session. It was as if he wanted to prove he was in control of the timing of the sessions. In this manic defense—turning the tables to show that he did not need me—it was as if he was saying, who is submissive now?

A sexualized feeling continued to pervade the sessions. Once, when Adam had the day off from work, he wore tight, flattering jeans to his session. He said he thought he caught me looking at his crotch. When I asked him how he felt about that, he said he was ambivalent. Partly, he liked the attention—especially that I would find him sexually attractive—but he also worried that I was judging him as cheap for wearing such tight jeans. It was clearly very important that I think highly of him, even though he had a poor impression of himself. Or maybe he wanted to excite me and have me see him as the bad boy who had chosen to wear tight jeans.

About a year into our work together, Adam began dating someone he had met at Alcoholics Anonymous. They went out for several months, and Adam was quite smitten. He described their sex as different from his usual type of S&M. The sex was more tender and loving, with neither person being degraded. After only four months, the other man dropped him suddenly, saying he simply did not feel as close to Adam as Adam evidently felt about him.

The breakup of the relationship devastated Adam. I imagined him like a puppy licking his wounds. I had a fantasy of gathering him in my arms and protecting him. During one session, he began to cry that he would never meet anyone again. I felt particularly close to him, which must have been evident and also very frightening to him. "I feel as though you're feeling sorry for me," he said. "That makes me feel weak, that you are dominant. I'm the slave and you're the master. It's both scary and very exciting." During this period, Adam had the following dream: "You aggressively pursue me to have sex. You're on top. Your balls and pubic hair are shaven. I lick you."

Adam's associations were that he had to have sex with me to please me. He was angry that he had to follow my rules, that I was "on top." Yet, in waking life, he finds smooth balls exciting. However, he also associated to a TV show about a rapist with shaven testicles. Adam had mixed feelings about my being a rapist in his dream. Rapists force you to do sexual things you do not want to do, but at the same time being raped was similar to his sexual fantasies.

In the dream and his associations, Adam was expressing great conflict in his experience of me as a sexual partner. He was angry at having to follow my rules and experienced me as a rapist, but this anger did not stop him from being excited by me and licking me. The dream went hand in hand with Adam's taking on a more assertive role, as he pressed me to find out more about my personal life. Was I gay? In a relationship? What kind of sex did I like? His questions had an entitled, demanding quality that made me hesitate to answer them. I told him my reaction on at least one occasion, and at other times I did not answer him directly, at least not at first, but instead explored his fantasies. He often reacted by becoming annoyed, saying he hated it when I was in control. And yet, unlike the dream, I experienced him in the role of the active pursuer. Suddenly I felt in the one-down position, which made me a little uncomfortable. Things did not seem particularly sexual; rather, they had a compulsory quality.

Several sessions later, my discomfort increased as Adam delightedly announced that he wanted to be the one to cause the emotional pain in our relationship for a change. He felt that our roles had reversed: he was in charge now, and I had to serve him. He found this exciting. He reported another dream: "You were in a wheelchair. You couldn't walk yet you still seemed very powerful to me, even though you were fragile. You were older than you are, too. But, then again, I was in control. I finally got to push you around."

There were many elements to this rich and complex dream. I resonated with the image of how frail I was, even as I was powerful; how, by pushing me around, Adam was also taking care of me, a familiar role from his childhood. Adam's associations were to pushing me around as a way of being in control. I wondered why we needed to split roles, with only one of us being in control and why Adam needed to disassociate being strong from being a caretaker.

But while Adam agreed that the dream was more complex than he thought, he seemed bent on seeing that his version of pushing me around came to fruition in the treatment. He soon announced that he had returned to "barebacking," sometimes being the receptive partner during condomless anal sex. It made him feel powerful and invincible not to need a rubber—that was as close as he could get to another man without anything standing in his way. I saw his powerful associations to unsafe, anonymous sex as a defense against feelings of vulnerability. He was acting as if he were not at risk for AIDS and other sexually transmitted diseases—or of too much closeness with me. I also sensed that he was expressing great anger at his father by metaphorically screaming, "See what I have to do to win your attention." I also felt that he was expressing anger toward me for being the one in control for so long.

Over the next several months, I walked a tightrope trying to figure out how to respond to Adam and his unsafe sex. I felt very uncomfortable with what he was doing, and I told him so in no uncertain terms. I wondered why he was willing to take such a risk with his life. Adam felt it was a risk worth taking, since he always asked his partner about his HIV status before having sex with him. I still considered this playing Russian roulette since there was no way of knowing whether his anonymous partner was lying or even knew his HIV status for certain.

There was so much I wanted to understand about why Adam had suddenly decided to bareback, but I could hear the clock ticking. I realized there was a connection between his risky behavior outside the treatment and within. He seemed unconcerned about how I would respond, just as he was unconcerned about the dangers of his behavior; in fact, he seemed sadistically to be enjoying my discomfort. Just as his health hung in the balance, so too did the treatment. How was what was going on between us connected to the sexual feelings he was having toward me and his feeling that our roles had reversed and he was now on top? I now knew what it was like to be Adam in a relationship—to feel inferior, humiliated, at the mercy of the other. I needed to find some way to communicate this understanding empathically while I was still feeling angry and powerless.

I had several choices. I could take the hardest line possible and insist that, if we were to work together, Adam would have to stop barebacking. But to make this demand risked Adam's bolting the treatment or simply not telling me he was having sex without condoms. Or I could analyze what was going on between us as I would any other enactment, but doing this seemed inadequate to the great risk involved. How would I communicate to Adam my surprise and great concern for what he was doing to his health while also trying to understand analytically what was going on to cause it?

I decided to share my quandary with Adam. I told him I was trying to be open-minded and nonjudgmental, but I was finding it difficult to understand why he was making the decisions he was making at that point in time. I was at a loss to know how to respond to him; I realized that, if I came down too hard, I would only be reestablishing what he experienced as my being in control and his being in the weak, humiliated position. But I wondered if that was the position he wanted me to occupy. I worried that he was enjoying my discomfort but that it was really himself that he was hurting. Mostly, I was deeply worried for his health and safety and hoped that what I said sounded as if it came from that place.

Adam seemed touched by how agonized I was trying to find a way to respond to him. It was nice not to be the only vulnerable person in the relationship, he said. He added that there was a part of him that also felt uncomfortable about barebacking. He admitted to having sexual feelings toward me that he worried would not be reciprocated and that this likelihood seemed to be another injustice. So what I said about his being angry with me might be true. He made no promises to use condoms all the time, but he agreed to continue talking about the subject.

Over the next couple of weeks, Adam and I engaged in an awkward dance around his condom use. For a while, he told me that he was, in fact, using condoms, and I believed him. During this time, we looked at how frightening it was to be vulnerable. We made connections to his childhood, including the times he saw his naked father take a strap to his brother and how Adam had felt a little excited and also jealous. Having sex without a condom was certainly one way to be a bad boy and hope to get his father's attention. I wondered if he felt he could not get my attention unless he was truly as bad as he could be. Was I another person he experienced as willing to see only the good-boy sides of him—the sides that free-associated, were introspective, brought in interesting dreams, and did not make too many waves?

"No," he said, "I think you see more of me than almost any other person does. But I think you're such a goody-goody yourself that it makes me want to shock you and get to see some of your other sides."

I remembered when Adam asked me what kind of sex I had and now realized he must have assumed it was quite staid compared with his. This discrepancy might have again left him feeling better than I, or worse. I wondered aloud if he assumed that I would be the kind of person who always wore a condom and if my doing so made him feel competitively that he wanted to have sex without them.

"I never thought of that," Adam said. "But there may be something to it."

For several more weeks, Adam and I talked about his fantasy that my life was both dull but also more intimate than his. According to Adam, we both had reason to be jealous of the other. We also talked about Adam's finding danger to be exciting. He liked speeding his bicycle through New York traffic, for instance. Yet throughout this period he continued to use condoms.

But, after a while, Adam told me that he had begun to have unprotected anal sex again. I was both angry and concerned, and I told him so. Adam responded that I should not treat him like a child. I asked how I should treat him when he was acting so irresponsibly. I was taking his decision as a personal rebuke. Had he meant it that way, or was I taking it too personally?

And then Adam came in with the news: he had tested HIV-positive. We were both devastated. The good news was that the infection had been caught early, and he had plenty of medication options. Somehow this seemed like a hollow victory. We were both left to live with a list of what-ifs. What if I had been more emphatic, insisting on a "condom-only rule"? What if I had given him more space, rather than entering an S&M enactment and feeling as if he were slapping me around? I realized only then how responsible I felt for Adam's behavior.

I was guilt-ridden because I had not been able to prevent his infection. In my more grandiose moments, I even felt as if I had caused his infection by being too relaxed and inconsistent about his unsafe sex. My sense of responsibility—having to be the good, hardworking analyst—directly paralleled Adam's experience that he had to be hyperresponsible in his own life.

Adam was also filled with self-recrimination. He was particularly concerned that I was angry at him and would no longer want to work with him. Adam was right about my anger. I was angry with him for getting infected, for not listening to me, for making me feel so powerless.

Adam and I had much to process, and we did so as best we could. I shared my feelings of anger, and we both talked about our guilt. We forgave each other. There was a sense that nothing could be done now except to accept what had happened or be eaten up by what we had done wrong.

The bottom line was that we could live in the what-ifs or in the present. Adam was HIV-positive. What mattered now was keeping him healthy without infecting anybody else or getting reinfected himself by having further unsafe sex.

And so we continued. As we both openly shared our feelings, for the first time, Adam did not experience me as being in the one-up or one-down position, but rather as another person in a relationship for whom he could have tender feelings. He realized that I had not abandoned him, even when I was angry at him, and I would not abandon him now when he needed me. Despite all my uncertainties, I had somehow survived Adam's aggression and thus made it possible for him to enter the Winnicottian (1969) stage of object usage, or what we today consider intersubjectivity (Benjamin, 1990). He again began to ask personal questions, but this time they seemed less prying and more that he simply wanted to know me better. He was curious to know if I was in a relationship. How did I handle it? Did I have to struggle with sex and sexuality? Did I share his spirituality? And, most important, was I worried about him?

I answered most of Adam's questions. Sometimes I explored their meaning before I answered; sometimes I waited to hear his associations until after I gave him my answer (as when I told him I certainly did worry about him). As I wrote these words, I noted that the last two times I typed Adam's name, I had slipped and used his real name rather than his pseudonym. It is a shame that it took Adam's getting sick for both of us to find each other in the most human terms, rather than solely as a partner in domination and submission.

When Adam terminated nine months later, his health was good, his prognosis excellent. He had joined an HIV support group and had begun dating one the members. As we hugged, our good-bye was a far cry from the first weeks of treatment when Adam was determined not to pay five dollars more than was necessary, and power and humiliation were such important themes.

Adam and I were fortunate to be able to work through our feelings about his contracting the AIDS virus. For, regardless of the circumstances, when a patient becomes HIV-positive during treatment, thorny questions are raised about the limitations of the analyst's role. How realistic is it to assume that transference organizes a person's outside life as much as it organizes the treatment? Whether we like it or not, our patients have their own lives to live regardless of how we think they should best live them.

Adam taught me the importance of being aware of my prejudices and of not making assumptions. I had presumed that the kind of S&M sex he enjoyed was by definition pathological. Those dynamics repeated issues from his childhood and created problems as they played out in other areas of his life. When it came to sex, however, I learned that domination and submission could be a surprisingly mutual, even healthy, experience. Adam surprised me in many ways: by combining wholesome looks with a secret sex life, by being willing to risk his life for an omnipotent sense of freedom. But the greatest surprise of all was what I learned about myself: that I could find his sexual activities exciting, even if I never engaged in them. And that revelation packed quite a punch.

10

THE GAY ANALYST
Different Populations,
Unique Dilemmas

Several years ago, when I was seeking a new supervisor, I consulted with an analyst who had written an important early paper on homosexuality. I had no idea whether or not the man was gay, and at first I thought it did not much matter to me. So I was surprised when, after making the appointment to meet with him, I began having a fantasy that he was, in fact, gay. Working as a therapist can be an isolating experience and working as a gay therapist is even more so. After having been analyzed by straight analysts, supervised by straight supervisors, and instructed by primarily (or at least presumably) straight teachers, advisers, and authors, I found myself thinking how nice it would be to have a gay mentor. Not that I have felt misunderstood or not accepted by any of my therapists, supervisors, or teachers. Just different.

So in my fantasy I imagined the unique commonality, bordering on a magical understanding, that gay Dr. H and I would share. He would know just what it is like to grow up feeling that there is something very different, and wrong, about you; to feel a flush of shame when a relative who "doesn't know" asks why you have not met a nice girl and settled down yet; to have seen too many people die of AIDS before age 40.

And so I became eager to meet with Dr. H, to whom I had already assigned a sexual orientation, a personal history, and an outlook on the world that were, coincidentally, just like my own. So imagine my surprise during my consultation when, in response to my direct question, he informed me that he was a practicing heterosexual.

Not that there's anything wrong with that.

As it turns out, Dr. H impressed me and I decided to enter supervision with him. But I found myself thinking about the assumptions I had been making—what they meant about me as a person and as an analyst and what they might tell me about my patients and our work together. That experience led me to wonder about other clinical questions as well. For example, what specific countertransference reactions are likely to be activated in me as a gay man, as *this* gay man? How are the reactions of this gay analyst shaped by the gender, sexual orientation, and personality structure of a particular patient? And what general principles of psychoanalytic theory and praxis can be elaborated when one asks these questions from a "queer" perspective? These are just some of the questions the case presentations in this volume are meant to address.

Gay and lesbian analysts find themselves in a unique position. Although much is changing, we live in a society and practice a profession that is heterosexist at best and homophobic at worst.[1] For

---

[1]David Schwartz (1993) has coined the term heterophilia to connote the "overvaluing of intimate relations between different-sexed partners" (p. 643), as when a therapist asks a gay patient whether he uses condoms but does not ask a straight patient.

example, the lively and often contentious social debate about gay marriage clearly illustrates how threatening it can be to see gay men and lesbians stake a claim for true equality. Similarly, it is only since the 1990s that gay men, lesbians, and bisexuals have been able to come comfortably out of the closet at psychoanalytic institutes. (Drescher, 1995; Martin, 1995; Isay, 1996; Blechner, 1996; Magee and Miller, 1997).

If sexuality has the power to destabilize (Davies, 2004), then homosexuality has the ability to create shock waves; it therefore must be subjugated. Patriarchal society privileges male heterosexuality (Foucault, 1976, Dimen, 2003). Psychoanalysis' hierarchy of sexual values (Drescher, 1998) "perpetuate[s] an ancient but official story that heterosexual genital sexuality (penile–vaginal intercourse) is the highest form of adult sexuality" (p. 217). From this hierarchical perspective, nonprocreative expressions of sexuality are often labeled perversions. Gayle Rubin (1982) writes:

> Marital, reproductive heterosexuals are alone at the top of the erotic pyramid. Clamoring below are unmarried monogamous heterosexuals and couples, followed by most other heterosexuals. Solitary sex floats ambiguously. . . . Stable, long-term lesbian and gay male couples are verging on respectability, but bar dykes and promiscuous gay men are hovering just above the groups at the very bottom of the pyramid. The most despised sexual casts currently include transsexuals, transvestites, fetishists, sadomasochists, sex workers such as prostitutes and porn models, and the lowliest of all, those whose eroticism transgresses generational boundaries [pp. 11–12].

As a result of these embedded values, growing up gay in our society means that one is saddled with a sense of difference and shame (Frommer, 1994, 1995; Blum and Pfetzing, 1997; Drescher, 1998). Members of other oppressed groups can at least turn to their families, their communities, and religious institutions for a sense of confirmation, recognition, and affirmation. However, gay youth, who may sense something different and dangerous about themselves from as early as age four (Isay, 1989; Phillips, 2002), must hide their sexuality from the very people who otherwise would most support them. A sense of being an alien in one's own family is all the more poignant because gay youth cannot label the nature of their difference or turn to their parents for understanding. On the contrary, they must hide their confusing differences at all costs:

> A sense of "feeling different" is difficult enough, but when one intuitively senses that it might be related to some of the most taboo, frightening, despised images in our culture, as well as in one's own family, then this is surely too emotionally over stimulating as well as cognitively disorganizing for the young proto-gay child. . . . It also highlights the mutually incompatible experiences of self in relation to other: the boy who feels generally valued and approved of in his family, who hears his parents viciously talk about "faggots," and who experiences, in very confusing ways, primitive discomfort and withdrawal by his father from him, at unexplained moments, repeated over and over again [Blum and Pfetzing, 1997, p. 433].

As a result, a gay boy splits off and dissociates his sexuality; he grows up with a sense of himself as damaged and his sexuality as something that must be hidden. Themes around secrets and the desire to be known often become paramount. Wishes to be accepted, to be found worthwhile, to have one's true self recognized and affirmed take place against the backdrop of internalized homophobia and the desire to keep one's homosexuality from those who might disapprove. Many gay and lesbian therapists with whom I have spoken talk about how much more relaxed they feel working with homosexual clients.

Isay (1991) has warned of the "always present countertransference need to use one's gay patients to counter the sense of professional isolationism" (p. 211). How times have changed. Now there are organizations for gay and lesbian psychiatrists (Association of Gay and Lesbian Psychiatrists; Gay and Lesbian Psychiatrists of New York) and psychologists (Division 44 of the American Psychological Association), as well as for Gay and Lesbian Analysts (GALA). I supervise at an institute founded by an openly lesbian analyst (Psychoanalytic Psychotherapy Study Center); a second (National Institute for the Psychotherapies) added coursework in gender and sexuality, and another (Contemporary Center for Advanced Psychoanalytic Studies at Fairleigh Dickinson University) now encourages its faculty to bring their "significant others," rather than their "husbands and wives," to institute events. It is difficult to believe that it has been less than two decades since a gay colleague at a classical institute told me he had no intention of coming out even in supervision for fear that he would be expelled.

Yet, for all that has changed, some things remain the same. While there are more openly gay candidates in analytic institutes and the institutes themselves are far more welcoming, being gay in the psychoanalytic world can still be an isolating experience. Professional conferences are often segregated; those on gender and sexuality feature gay and lesbian speakers, and conferences on other subjects mostly do not. Heterosexual analysts may refer gay patients to gay analysts, but they may be less willing to think of a gay or lesbian colleague when referring a heterosexual patient. In other words, heterosexism is still very much alive and well in psychoanalysis. It is just more neatly tucked in around the edges—which makes it all the more insidious.

Little wonder that examples of heterosexism sometimes seep into my clinical work. As the previous chapters show, my subjectivity as a gay analyst, and as a gay man in general, is always present in the room. It plays out differently, however, depending on the patient. What follows is a summation of some of the key issues that surfaced in my work with the eight patients I have described. Whether struggling with my fear about being outed by a heterosexual client, engaging in a homoerotic countertransference with a gay man, or basking in a fantasy of being a female patient's husband and father to her child, my countertransference played an important role in each treatment.

Summation of Key Issues

Chapter 3: Big Boys Don't Cry

In his effeminate presentation, José challenged my postmodernist beliefs. Although I am in agreement with those theorists who put forth that both gender and sexual orientation are socially constructed (Foucault, 1976; Butler, 1990; Goldner, 1993; Lesser, 1995; Schwartz, 1995; D'Ercole, 1996; Schwartz, 1998), and especially with those who believe there is a dialectical tension between fluid constructions and fixed genders (Harris, 1991; Sweetnam, 1996; Layton, 1998; Dimen, 2003), José made me realize how reflexive it is to think in binary terms of masculine and feminine or gay and straight.

José did not possess the masculine traits I associated with manhood. In fact, he carried himself in a way that seemed more feminine than masculine. His posturing made me feel uncomfortable, that I, too, was not enough of a man, since I share José's sexual orientation and some of his history of being teased. In the countertransference, I was denying my connection to José by instead identifying with the tormentors—his classmates, teachers, and, of course, his father, who recoiled from him because of his effeminacy. I pulled away for fear that I would be identified with him. My withdrawal must have been obvious to José, who had grown used to people pulling back from him or trying to control him because they considered him weak and effeminate.

Boys who grow up with behaviors that are typically designated as feminine often meet with derision and are filled with shame (Drescher, 1998). It does not help when their therapists feel ashamed of them, as I initially did with José.

Corbett (1996) might have had José in mind when he wrote of a subset of homosexual boys he called "girlyboys." Girlyboys have been pathologized by psychologists and psychoanalysts for their interest in things normally considered feminine. Analysts have repeatedly posited a developmental course for boys who identify with their mothers that assumes some early trauma and forecasts poor ego development and maturational difficulties. Psychoanalytic theory does not allow for the possibility that a boy who adopts stereotypically feminine behavior could have his own masculine identity and that he might actually enjoy this gendered combination throughout his life.

It took me a while to realize that I was guilty of engaging in this kind of restrictive thinking with José. It was only when he was able to confront me (about my trying to stop his crying) or I was able to confront myself (about pulling away and becoming distracted) that I grew to like and respect my patient. In the process, I also grew to like my own more feminine side. By refusing to accept my discomfort with him, José helped me help him, and he also helped me help myself.

Chapter 4: Adventures in Suburbia

Swaggering Rich presented a similar quandary for me around stereotypical masculinity, although one that played out very differently. As with José, with Rich I equated homosexuality with a lack of masculinity and became concerned about what my being gay said about me. I became overly nervous that Rich would find out that I was gay; I countertransferentially conflated my homosexuality with not being enough of a man. Without realizing it, I had fallen into the theoretical and cultural trap of equating male homosexuality with femininity (Frommer, 1994; Lesser, 1995; Drescher, 1998). As Frommer (1994) writes:

> Homosexuals in our society, whether masculine or effeminate in their appearance, are perceived as feminine because they have sex with other men, a behavior that is female-identified.

Male analysts are not immune to anxiety and shame about the passive, feminine aspects of their character, which are necessary ingredients to doing analytic work [p. 229].

That Rich might not care about my sexual orientation—or that he might have experienced it in more positive ways—became irrelevant as we entered into power struggles around who could be more of a "man." These altercations were a form of "reversible complementarity" in which the mutual recognition of intersubjectivity breaks down into a sadomasochistic power struggle (Benjamin, 1988, 1999; Ipp, 2002).

I initially engaged in such fights partly because I felt goaded by Rich, but also because I was bent on proving my masculinity to him (and to myself). If I "fought like a man," he might not question my sexual orientation. I did not stop to ask myself what would be so terrible if he found out I was gay. In retrospect, I was afraid he would belittle me, as had the kids who called me names when I was growing up.

Although I believe some good work took place with a very difficult patient, I realize the treatment ended prematurely, partly because of my fears of being less of a man in Rich's eyes, as well as in my own.

Chapter 5: Erotic Countertransference
With Heterosexual Patients

The Boy with the Hair. The danger of being found out as gay and unacceptable also permeated my work with Jim. If Rich represented the heterosexual who would beat me up if he discovered I was gay, Jim was the heterosexual who would sever all ties if he found that I had feelings for him—or that he had feelings for me. Like that of many gay men, my history includes the painful rejection by an all-important heterosexual man—my father—in part because of my sexual orientation. Straight men like Jim reawaken that fear of retraumatization, as I find myself dampening sexual feelings to make them safer.

I do not know if Jim surmised that I was gay and found him attractive, but this realization certainly would have filled him with terror. The idea of getting close to *anyone* was terrifying enough. Guntrip (1969) notes that the analyst's presence as another person who can disappoint the patient creates an anxiety so great that the therapist must be kept at arm's length. Through projective identification, Jim recreated his unavailable mother (and father) by lolling me into sleepiness and keeping me at a distance. I believe I felt Jim's voracious neediness underneath his depression, and I may have withdrawn from this, afraid it would be too much for me (a fear Jim may have also had about his neediness). Finally, my sleepiness may have been a way to deny my attraction to this straight man, an attraction that seemed dangerous, given Jim's sexual orientation and my own issues around rejection and being found out.

A Time to Flirt. Unlike with Jim, Melissa's fear of abandonment—and not my own—was an important theme of the treatment. I was aware of my role in an enactment: I played the part of the boyfriend/father who Melissa hoped would finally recognize her as an attractive, intelligent young woman, but who might once again leave her feeling abandoned. Unlike the other men in her life, I showed an interest in her without using her or casting her aside. At the same time, I truly was one of the unattainable men to whom Melissa was attracted. "Passing" as straight, I felt a little as though I were leading her on, lying, or at the very least hiding the truth. I knew that one of Melissa's strongest unrequited crushes had been on a gay man. Furthermore, I felt guilty that I enjoyed coming across as heterosexual. Was I not proud of being gay? Yet I felt my homosexuality had to be kept a secret, as if I were an adolescent again.

Nevertheless, I enjoyed our mutual flirtation. I even took pleasure in being a gay man mistaken for a heterosexual one. The ability to pass as straight meant I did not have to worry that I fit an effeminate gay stereotype, as José did. What is more, I reveled in the transferential ability to turn a woman on. I felt attractive, worthy, sexual—as Melissa must have felt about herself. But more than that, I felt accepted as a straight man, and there was something strangely rewarding about that acceptance. At least twice a week for 45 minutes I got a small taste of how the other 90 percent lives. Fortunately, I did not act on my feelings, although I could see how an analyst might have been tempted to break a sexual boundary with Melissa (Gabbard and Lester, 2002). I would not consciously want to trade my gay life for anything, but it is nice to live a heterosexual fantasy every once in a while.

Chapter 6: And Baby Makes Three

It was every bit as fulfilling to pretend to be both husband and father to Deborah and Nicole as it was to pass for straight with Melissa. The only problem was, I did not act as if I were pretending. My desire to have a traditional heterosexual family was so great that I colluded with Deborah to allow her to bring her daughter to session for seven months, even though clinically I knew this was a mistake.

While there is, of course, no reason that as a gay man I cannot become a father, I still felt the pull of living the "acceptable" heterosexual life, complete with a loving wife and child. For a gay man in our society there is still always the feeling of being an outsider, unable to enjoy all the privileges of conventional heterosexuality. Whenever I fill out any form asking my marital status, I have to check the box that says "single" even though I have been partnered for 10 years to a man with whom I share a home and my life as any married couple does.

My work with Deborah brings to mind the gay men I have treated who did choose the closeted route of heterosexual marriage and sometimes fatherhood. Feelings of isolation and loneliness, concerns about one's career and social standing, the need to please family, and a fear of growing old, lonely, and sexually desperate—these are the usual reasons why gay men and lesbians, particularly those of a certain age, marry heterosexually (Isay, 1996; Drescher, 1998). I always feel sad for everyone involved in these situations, and I realize there is a big difference between my fantasy of being married and the actuality of doing it. I consider myself lucky to have grown up in a time (the 1960s and 70s), in a place (New York City), and in a family where at least one parent (my mother) was accepting of my homosexuality. And, of course, I have worked on myself and my biases in supervision and in analysis. But there remained enough heterosexism in me to have a fantasy of marrying Deborah and being the father of her child until I woke up to the enactment and found a way to bring her anger into the treatment.

Chapter 7: The Analyst Falls Asleep

With Deborah, I had to struggle with internalized heterosexism that had me fantasizing about being straight. With Steve, much of the homophobia resided within him. The result was his own desire to be heterosexual, or, since this was not possible, at least to be asexual.

Steve was one of three patients I reported on (José and Jim being the others) who, I felt, pushed me away and therefore I became sleepy. Steve, however, is the only patient in one of those sessions I have actually fallen asleep. I believe there were many causes for this enactment, one being my frustration at Steve's not wanting to talk about his sexuality, much less embrace it. I had many agendas for my ambivalent patient—to get him to come to sessions on time, to get him to talk about his feelings, and, mostly, to get him to embrace (and act on) his sexual orientation. I believe the last is a common countertransference reaction for gay therapists working with self-hating gay patients. The analyst must walk a fine line between pushing his own agenda and unshackling the patient from his shame so that the patient is free to choose the way he wants to express his sexuality.

Steve dreaded entering into an intimate relationship with another man, specifically with another gay man—me. Yet Steve's secret desire was to be known and penetrated by me (Ghent, 1990). By falling asleep, however, I may have ended up enacting the deadness and denial of his desire in his inner world (Ogden, 1995). My falling asleep may have been a response to erotic feelings shared by both of us. I became Sleeping Beauty, awaiting a kiss from Prince Charming to awaken me. Then, too, was I afraid that things would get too rough between us—afraid of both his buried aggressiveness and my own?

In Steve's refusal to talk about my falling asleep, we were reenacting an aspect of his sexual fantasy in the way that he tied my hands. In the countertransference, I felt frustrated and excluded. I had to remind myself that this *was* Steve's way of inviting me into his inner world.

My falling asleep was a complicated enactment with multiple meanings. That Steve and I could both work our ways through it, and, in fact, grow from the experience, shows the potential benefits of enactments when the analyst becomes aware of and is prepared to analyze them.

Chapter 8: Homoerotic Countertransference

Interestingly, while *I* became sleepy with Steve, the situation was reversed with Kevin. It was he who entered a foggy, dissociated state when I mentioned that we had both been avoiding his sexuality. My comment may have overwhelmed him, causing the grogginess that would remain throughout the rest of the session. This type of dissociation is also typical of patients who survived childhood sexual abuse but were unable to integrate the overwhelming experience (Davies and Frawley, 1992, 1994), as was the case with Kevin and his stepfather. Finally, the sleepiness may have been a way to keep me—and the subject of Kevin's sexuality—at a distance, even as he dared to introduce it by bringing in the photograph of himself in a bathing suit.

As I have written elsewhere (Sherman, 2002a,b), enactments can be particularly charged when they involve two men in the analytic dyad, especially when both men are gay. Had I continued to ignore the erotic material in my work with Kevin, my avoidance might have further contributed to his sense of shame and avoidance, thus increasing the chance that the feelings would continue to be driven underground. In contrast, my playing with homoerotic stirrings in the countertransference with Kevin, including struggling with ways to understand and express them, created an atmosphere of safety for the patient to introduce and integrate split-off aspects of his self (Dimen, 1999).

This was much easier for me to do with Kevin than with heterosexual Jim (whom I actually found more attractive) because I felt I did not have to worry about being found out. Kevin knew that I was gay, and there was something safe and at the same time enlivening about his knowing. I looked forward to my sessions with Kevin as if each were the premiere of a Broadway show I had been waiting to see for months. The work had a sense of immediacy and spontaneity, and I felt relaxed and in control, even as my countertransference feelings changed, within minutes, from feeling excited to feeling dirty.

In some ways, Kevin is typical of gay and lesbian youngsters who grow up unable to integrate an affirmative sexual identity. In Kevin's case, however, his difficulties in sexual-identity development were compounded by the early, furtive, sexualized relationship with his stepfather. In general, however, societal and familial signals that stigmatize homosexuality usually generate feelings of shame, humiliation, confusion, and lack of masculinity, particularly during adolescence (Frommer, 1994; Drescher, 1998). For some gay youth (and later, adults), sex often becomes compartmentalized and split off from the rest of the self as charged desires come to seem perverted, threatening, needing to be denied or avoided. Lewes (1998) even describes a category of gay men for whom embarrassment and humiliation can themselves become sources of erotic excitement: "They may attempt to exorcise feelings of shame at sexual arousal by adopting the role of flouter of social convention or of sexual outlaw. Blatantly indecent behavior or extreme promiscuity is the characteristic of both stances" (pp. 355–356).

In a commentary on my original paper about Kevin (Sherman, 2002a), Frommer (2002) notes how my countertransferential feelings shifted so quickly from excitement to shame as I picked up on Kevin's ambivalence about sex with his stepfather. It made Kevin feel dirty, but it was also exciting. Coming at a time when he was first exploring his sexual interest in men, Kevin conflated shame about his unrecognized victimization with shame about same-sex desire. This ambivalence was enacted with me when I felt excited by Kevin's boyish sexuality but also ashamed of myself for having this response. Frommer further notes that Kevin and I were stuck in complementary sex roles: the patient in the role of "bad" boy and I in the role of choirboy. Both of Frommer's interpretations illustrate how Kevin might have split love and lust in his life. Although Kevin had a hard time having loving, sexual feelings toward his partner, he enjoyed having sadomasochistic sex with strangers.

Chapter 9: When Push Comes to Shove

While some of Kevin's sadomasochistic activities, particularly eating out of his partner's anus, made me feel uncomfortable, I was initially excited and fascinated by Adam's world of submission and domination. Both Kevin and Adam accused me of having a bland sex life, although both felt I had the kind of intimate relationship for which they longed. Yet they were not the only ones who were jealous. I found myself intoxicated by the mutuality, the sense of recognition and affirmation involved in Adam's rough sexual play with a willing partner. I like to think I do not shock easily when patients describe their sex lives. But I did not realize how much I would enjoy hearing about sexual practices that I would have considered deviant under other circumstances.

When working with gay patients, I try not to be judgmental about lifestyle choices that are different from my own. However, I value relationships, monogamy, and more traditional expressions of sexual intimacy. Therefore, it is always a challenge to keep an open mind when I am working with a patient who states he is not interested in a monogamous relationship and whose sexual interests are raunchier than my own. In fact, I could not entirely avoid judging Adam for his interest in sadomasochistic sex. Yet I nevertheless found myself excited to hear about his exploits. This excitement reflected, in part, my willingness to be open to his experience. Adam was so sweet, charming, and hardworking that it was difficult (at least at first) not to like him, no matter what he was doing in the bedroom. However, there may have been an element of a sexualized defense against my own discomfort with the activities he was describing.

For both Kevin and Adam, domination and submission represented attempts to work through childhood developmental conflicts and traumas, as was the case in both their relationships with other men and in the transference (Weille, 2002). For Adam, the son of an abusive, sexually humiliating father and a depressed mother, masochism was a "search for recognition through another who is powerful enough to bestow that recognition" (Benjamin, 1988, p. 56). Engaging in "dirty" sex was enjoyable because it was one of the few times Adam did not need to present a compliant, "good-boy" false self (Winnicott, 1960). Instead, the patient was able vicariously to get in touch with his own power through his dominating partner (Bader, 1993).

That is what happened in the enactment around killing the fly. At first, Adam played the role of masochist exclusively in his outside life and with me, a role he had learned in his childhood at the hands of his violent father. It was when he could experience me as a playful partner, getting in touch with my own sadism toward the fly, that he could share with me more about his sex life and ultimately switch roles. But Adam's sadism did not seem entirely playful to me. It seemed to have a dangerous edge. Unlike the sharing of power in his domination and submission play, I felt that I was being abused as he tied my hands with his unsafe sex. Ultimately, Adam paid a high price and contracted HIV. Both of us were left feeling angry, afraid, and guilty. However, we were able to survive the devastating news and even grow from it.

Conclusion

Working in the countertransference is about finding ways to deepen the work so that the patient, and sometimes the analyst, ends up with a life that is richer and more fulfilling than before. As these case reports illustrate, the analyst cannot help but be a constant participant in the therapeutic endeavor.[2]

No matter how well analyzed, the therapist's core issues remain. To a gay analyst, this means being aware of the issues of hiding and revealing, pride and shame, to name a few. I have tried to illustrate that the emergence of these and other issues in treatment does not necessarily portend disaster. In fact, such moments can be put to good use and can be a turning point in the therapy. It is crucial, however, that the therapist be in, or have been in, a good-enough analysis of his own. Good supervision is also important. But, in the final analysis, with all the other ghosts in the room (our analysts, our supervisors, our parents, society, the profession) there are only two people spending 45 minutes together in one of the most intimate of all relationships. It takes courage on the part of both patient and analyst to withstand the anxiety of a sometimes painful intimacy in session after session. It certainly requires bravery to discuss with colleagues—in supervision, in our literature, and at our conferences—how we really are and what we really do with our patients when we are behind closed doors.

_____

[2]See Sullivan's (1953) concept of participant observer.

REFERENCES

Altman, N. (1996), *The Analyst in the Inner City: Race, Class, and Culture Through a Psychoanalytic Lens*. Hillsdale, NJ: The Analytic Press.

_____ (2000), Black and white thinking: A psychoanalyst reconsiders race. *Psychoanal. Dial.,* 10:589–605.

Aron, L. (1991), The patient's experience of the analyst's subjectivity. *Psychoanal. Dial.,* 1:29–51.

_____ (1992), Interpretation as expression of the analyst's subjectivity. *Psychoanal. Dial.,* 2:475–507

_____ (1996), *A Meeting of Minds: Mutuality in Psychoanalysis*. Hillsdale, NJ: The Analytic Press.

Bacal, H. A. & Thomson, P. G. (1996), The psychoanalyst's selfobject needs and the effect of their frustration on the treatment: A new view of countertransference. In: *Basic Ideas Reconsidered: Progress in Self Psychology, Vol. 12,* ed. A. Goldberg. Hillsdale, NJ: The Analytic Press, pp. 3–16.

Bader, M. J. (1993), Adaptive sadomasochism and psychological growth. *Psychoanal. Dial.,* 3:279–300.

Bass, A. (2003), "E" enactments in psychoanalysis: Another medium, another message. *Psychoanal. Dial.,* 13:657–675.

Benedek, T. (1953), Dynamics of the countertransference. *Bull. Menn. Clin.,* 17:201–239.

Benjamin, J. (1988), *The Bonds of Love.* New York: Random House.

———— (1990), Recognition and destruction: An outline of intersubjectivity. *Psychoanal. Psychol.,* 7(Suppl.):33–47.

———— (1999), Afterword to recognition and destruction: An outline of intersubjectivity. In: *Relational Psychoanalysis: The Emergence of a Tradition,* ed. S. Mitchell & L. Aron. Hillsdale, NJ: The Analytic Press, pp. 201–210.

Bion, W. R. (1959), Attacks on linking. *Internat. J. Psycho-Anal.,* 40:308–315.

Black, M. J. (2003), Enactment: Analytic musings on energy, language, and personal growth. *Psychoanal. Dial.,* 13:633–655.

Blechner, M. J. (1996), Psychoanalysis in and out of the closet. In: *The Therapist as a Person,* ed. B. Gerson. Hillsdale, NJ: The Analytic Press, pp. 223–239.

Blum, A. & Pfetzing, V. (1997), Assaults to the self: The trauma of growing up gay. *Gender & Psychoanal.,* 2:427–442.

Bollas, C. (1983), Expressive uses of the countertransference. *Contemp. Psychoanal.,* 19:1–34.

———— (1987), *The Shadow of the Object: Psychoanalysis of the Unthought Known.* New York: Columbia University Press.

Butler, J. (1990), *Gender Trouble.* New York: Routledge.

Chused, J. (1991), The evocative power of enactments. *J. Amer. Psychoanal. Assn.,* 39:615–639.

———— (2003), The role of enactments. *Psychoanal. Dial.,* 13:677–687.

Corbett, K. (1996), Homosexual boyhood: Notes on girlyboys. *Gender & Psychoanal.,* 1:429–461.

Crowley, M. (1968), *The Boys in the Band.* New York: Samuel French.

Davies, J. M. (2004), The times we sizzle, and the times we sigh: The multiple erotics of arousal, anticipation, and release. Presented at Annual Conference of the National Institute for the Psychotherapies, New York City, February.

———— & Frawley, M. G. (1992), Dissociative processes and transference–countertransference paradigms in psychoanalytically oriented treatment of adult survivors of childhood sexual abuse. *Psychoanal. Dial.,* 2:5–36.

———— & ———— (1994), *Treating the Adult Survivor of Childhood Sexual Abuse: A Psychoanalytic Perspective.* New York: Basic Books.

D'Ercole, A. (1996), Postmodern ideas about gender and sexuality: The lesbian woman redundancy. *Psychoanal. & Psychother.*, 13:142–152.

Dimen, M. (1999), Between lust and libido: Sex, psychoanalysis, and the moment before. *Psychoanal. Dial.*, 9:415–440.

———— (2003), *Sexuality, Intimacy, Power.* Hillsdale, NJ: The Analytic Press.

Drescher, J. (1995), Anti-homosexual bias in training, In: *Disorienting Sexuality*, ed. T. Domenici & R. Lesser. New York: Routledge, pp. 227–241.

———— (1998), *Psychoanalytic Therapy and the Gay Man.* Hillsdale, NJ: The Analytic Press.

———— (2002), Put up your dukes: A discussion of Eric Sherman's *Adventures in Suburbia.* Presented at International Association for Relational Psychoanalysis and Psychotherapy Conference, New York City, November.

Ehrenberg, D. B. (1992), *The Intimate Edge.* New York: Norton.

Epstein, L. (1995), Self-disclosure and analytic space. *Contemp. Psychoanal.*, 31:229–236.

Ferenczi, S. (1931), *The Clinical Diary of Sándor Ferenczi*, ed. J. Dupont. Cambridge, MA: Harvard University Press, 1988.

———— (1933), Confusion of tongues between adults and the child, In: *Final Contributions to the Theory and Technique of Psychoanalysis*, ed. J. Rickman. London: Maresfield Reprints.

Foucault, M. (1976), *The History of Sexuality, Vol. 1*, trans. R. Hurley. New York: Pantheon, 1978.

Frank, K. (1997), The role of the analyst's inadvertent self-revelations. *Psychoanal. Dial.*, 7:281–314.

———— (1999), *Psychoanalytic Participation: Action, Interaction, and Integration.* Hillsdale, NJ: The Analytic Press.

Freud, S. (1910), The future prospects of psychoanalytic therapy. *Standard Edition*, 11:141–151. London: Hogarth Press, 1957.

———— (1912), Recommendations to physicians practicing psychoanalysis. *Standard Edition*, 12:111–120. London: Hogarth Press, 1958.

Frommer, M. S. (1994), Homosexuality and psychoanalysis: Technical considerations revisited. *Psychoanal. Dial.*, 4:215–233.

———— (1995), Countertransference obscurity in the psychoanalytic treatment of homosexual patients. In: *Disorienting Sexuality*, ed. T. Domenici & R. Lesser. New York: Routledge, pp. 65–82.

———— (1999), Reflections on self-disclosure, desire, shame and emotional engagement in the gay male psychoanalytic dyad. *J. Gay & Lesbian Psychother.*, 3:53–65.

_____ (2002), Listening to the erotic: Commentary on paper by Eric Sherman. *Psychoanal. Dial.*, 12:675–686.

Gabbard, G. O. & Lester, E. P. (2002), *Boundaries and Boundary Violations in Psychoanalysis*. Washington, DC: American Psychiatric Press.

Ghent, E. (1990), Masochism, submission, surrender: Masochism as a perversion of surrender. *Contemp. Psychoanal.*, 26:108–135.

Goldner, V. (1993), Toward a critical relational theory of gender. *Psychoanal. Dial.*, 3:249–272.

Greenberg, J. (1991), Countertransference and reality. *Psychoanal. Dial.*, 1:52–73.

_____ (1995), Self-disclosure: Is it psychoanalytic? *Contemp. Psychoanal.*, 31:193–205.

Guntrip, H. (1969), *Schizoid Phenomenon, Object Relations and the Self*. New York: International Universities Press.

Harris, A. (1991), Gender as contradiction. *Psychoanal. Dial.*, 1:197–224.

Heimann, P. (1950), On countertransference. *Internat. J. Psycho-Anal.*, 31:81–84.

Hoffman, I. Z. (1991), Toward a social-constructivist view of the psychoanalytic situation. *Psychoanal. Dial.*, 1:74–105.

_____ (1994), Dialectical thinking and therapeutic action in the psychoanalytic process. *Psychoanal. Quart.*, 63:187–217.

Ipp, H. (2002), Commentary: Eric Sherman's case. Presented at International Association for Relational Psychoanalysis and Psychotherapy Conference, New York City, November.

Isay, R. A. (1989), *Being Homosexual: Gay Men and Their Development*. New York: Farrar, Straus & Giroux.

_____ (1991), The homosexual analyst: Clinical considerations. *The Psychoanalytic Study of the Child*, 46:199–216. New Haven, CT: Yale University Press.

_____ (1996), *Becoming Gay: The Journey to Self Acceptance*. New York: Pantheon.

Jacobs, T. J. (1986), On countertransference enactments. *J. Amer. Psychoanal. Assn.*, 34:289–307.

Joseph, B. (1989), *Psychic Equilibrium and Psychic Change*. London: Tavistock/Routledge.

Keren, M. S. (1999), Self-disclosure in the gay analyst straight patient dyad: A view from intersubjectivity. Presented at 22nd International Conference on the Psychology of the Self, Toronto, Canada, October.

Klein, M. (1946), Notes on some schizoid mechanisms. *Internat. J. Psycho-Anal.,* 33:433–438.

Lacan, J. (1977), *Écrits: A Selection,* trans. A. Sheridan. New York: Norton.

Layton, L. (1998), *Who's That Girl? Who's That Boy? Clinical Practice Meets Postmodern Gender Theory.* Hillsdale, NJ: The Analytic Press, 2004.

Leary, K. (2000), Racial enactments in dynamic treatment. *Psychoanal. Dial.,* 10:439–653.

Lesser, R. C. (1995), Objectivity as masquerade. In: *Disorienting Sexuality,* ed. T. Domenici & R. Lesser. New York: Routledge, pp. 83–96.

Levenson, E. (1972), *The Fallacy of Understanding.* New York: Basic Books.

———— (1983), *The Ambiguity of Change: An Inquiry into the Nature of Psychoanalytic Reality.* New York: Basic Books.

Lewes, K. (1998), A special oedipal mechanism in the development of male homosexuality. *Psychoanal. Psychol.,* 15:341–359.

Lewis, H. B. (1971), *Shame and Guilt in Neurosis.* New York: International Universities Press.

Linde, R. (1998), Discussion: Eros in a gay dyad. *Gender & Psychoanal.,* 3:347–353.

Little, M. (1951), Countertransference and the patient's response to it. *Internat. J. Psycho-Anal.,* 12:32–40.

———— (1957), "R"—The analyst's total response to his patient's needs. *Internat. J. Psycho-Anal.,* 38:240–254.

Magee, M. & Miller, D. (1997), *Lesbian Lives: Psychoanalytic Narratives Old and New.* Hillsdale, NJ: The Analytic Press.

Maroda, K. (1991), *The Power of Countertransference: Innovations in Analytic Technique.* Hillsdale, NJ: The Analytic Press, 2004.

Martin, A. (1995), A view from both sides: Coming out as a lesbian psychoanalyst. In: *Disorienting Sexuality,* ed. T. Domenici & R. Lesser. New York: Routledge, pp. 255–261.

Mitchell, S. A. (1988), *Relational Concepts in Psychoanalysis.* Cambridge, MA: Harvard University Press.

———— (1993), *Hope and Dread in Psychoanalysis.* New York: Basic Books.

———— (1997), *Influence and Autonomy in Psychoanalysis.* Hillsdale, NJ: The Analytic Press.

Ogden, T. (1994), *Subjects of Analysis.* Northvale, NJ: Aronson.

———— (1995), Analysing forms of aliveness and deadness of the transference–countertransference. *Internat. J. Psycho-Anal.,* 76:695–709.

Phillips, S. H. (1998), A new analytic dyad: Homosexual analyst, heterosexual patient. *J. Amer. Psychoanal. Assn.,* 46:1195–1219.

_____ (2002), The overstimulation of everyday life: II. Male homosexuality, countertransference, and psychoanalytic treatment. In: *The Annual of Psychoanalysis, Vol. 12: Rethinking Psychoanalysis and Homosexualities,* ed. J. Weiner, J. Anderson, B. Cohler & R. Shelby. Hillsdale, NJ: The Analytic Press.

Pick, I. (1985), Working through in the counter-transference. In: *Melanie Klein Today, Vol. 2,* ed. E. B. Spillius. London: Routledge, 1988, pp. 34–47.

Poland, W. S. (1984), On the analyst's neutrality. *J. Amer. Psychoanal. Assn.,* 32:283–299.

Racker, H. (1953), A contribution to the problem of countertransference. *Internat. J. Psycho-Anal.,* 34:313–324.

_____ (1957), The meanings and uses of countertransference. *Psychoanal. Quart.,* 26:303–357.

_____ (1968), *Transference and Countertransference.* New York: International Universities Press.

Renik, O. (1998), The role of countertransference enactment in successful clinical psychoanalysis. In: *Enactment: Toward a New Approach to the Therapeutic Relationship,* ed. S. J. Ellman & M. Moskowitz. Northvale, NJ: Aronson, pp. 111–128.

_____ (1999), Playing one's cards face up in analysis: An approach to the problem of self-disclosure. *Psychoanal. Quart.,* 68:521–539.

Rubin, G. (1982), Thinking sex. In: *The Lesbian and Gay Studies Reader,* ed. H. Abelove, M. A. Barale & D. Halperin. New York: Routledge, 1993, pp. 3–44.

Sandler, J. (1976), Countertransference and role-responsiveness. *Internat. Rev. Psycho-Anal.,* 3:43–47.

Schwartz, A. (1998), *Sexual Subjects: Lesbians, Gender and Psychoanalysis.* New York: Routledge.

Schwartz, D. (1993), Heterophilia: The love that dare not speak its aim. *Psychoanal. Dial.,* 3:643–652.

_____ (1995), Current psychoanalytic discourses on sexuality: Tripping over the body. In: *Disorienting Sexuality,* ed. T. Domenici & R. Lesser. New York: Routledge, pp. 115–126.

Searles, H. F. (1975), The patient as therapist to his analyst. In: *Tactics and Techniques of Psychoanalytic Therapy, Vol. II,* ed. P. Giovachini. New York: Aronson, pp. 95–151.

Sherman, E. (2002a), Homoerotic countertransference: The love that dare not speak its name? *Psychoanal. Dial.,* 12:649–666.

———— (2002b), Adventures in suburbia: The patient, the analyst, and the package in the waiting room. Presented at International Association for Relational Psychoanalysis and Psychotherapy Conference, New York City, November.

Spillius, E. B. (1988), *Melanie Klein Today, Vol. 2.* London: Routledge.

Stolorow, R. D. & Atwood, G. E. (1992), *Contexts of Being: The Intersubjective Foundations of Psychological Life.* Hillsdale, NJ: The Analytic Press.

Sullivan, H. S. (1953), *The Interpersonal Theory of Psychiatry.* New York: Norton.

Sweetnam, A. (1996), The changing contexts of gender: Between fixed and fluid experience. *Psychoanal. Dial.,* 6:437–459.

Symington, N. (1983), The analyst's act of freedom as agent of therapeutic change. *Internat. Rev. Psycho-Anal.,* 12:273–283.

Tower, L. E. (1956), Countertransference. *J. Amer. Psychoanal. Assn.,* 4: 224–255.

Weille, K. H. (2002), The psychodynamics of consensual sadomasochistic and dominant–submissive sexual games. *Studies Gender & Sexuality,* 3:131–160.

Winnicott, D. W. (1949), Hate in the countertransference. *Internat. J. Psycho-Anal.,* 30:69–75.

———— (1951), Transitional objects and transitional phenomena. In: *Playing and Reality.* London: Tavistock, 1971, pp. 1–25.

———— (1960), Ego distortion in terms of true and false self. In: *The Maturational Processes and the Facilitating Environment.* New York: International Universities Press, 1965, pp. 140–152.

———— (1969), The use of an object and relating through identifications. In: *Playing and Reality.* London: Tavistock, 1971, pp. 86–94.

INDEX

155